THE WRITER
ABROAD

THE WRITER ABROAD

Literary Travels from Austria
to Uzbekistan

Selected by Lucinda Hawksley

CONTENTS

NORTH AMERICA

CENTRAL AMERICA, SOUTH AMERICA, THE CARIBBEAN

THE POLES

AUSTRALASIA

INTRODUCTION

The 21st century sees people travelling more frequently than ever before. Places once considered impossibly remote have become popular as holiday resorts, and journeying to the other side of the world has become easier than travelling across a single country would have been in previous centuries. In our modern era of vlogs and blogs, texting and tweeting, few people make the effort to keep a travel journal, and far fewer even consider sitting down to write a letter to send home. *The Writer Abroad* looks back at a time when the pen was mightier than the trackpad, and to when travelling was an option only for the most adventurous – and the most privileged – of people.

Before the creation of fast planes, submarine trains, internet booking sites and electronic passports, travelling even a relatively short distance was an experience that required meticulous planning and great forethought. A journey to a distant town within one's home country was something that many people barely ever achieved. A journey to the other side of the same continent, let alone to another continent entirely, was considered a once-in-a-lifetime event. As such, these adventurous and arduous journeys were commemorated by the writing of minutely detailed letters and journals. The Writer Abroad uncovers the innermost thoughts and witty musings of historic travellers, from Herodotus to Roald Dahl. Discover what William Thackeray and Benjamin Franklin thought of Paris, what Dorothy Wordsworth recalled about her time in Scotland and how Harriet Martineau ended up in an Egyptian harem. Ponder Charlie Chaplin's experience of European trains, Mary Wollstonecraft's journey around Scandinavia, George Orwell's time in Marrakech, and what Ian Fleming might have been doing in Beirut. While working on this book I was taken on a journey not only around the globe, but also back in time. I discovered which building Marco Polo considered 'the greatest Palace that ever was', journeyed through Somalia with Sir Richard Burton and read the words of William Dampier from when he visited what is now Australia back in the 17th century. I found inspiration at Niagara Falls with Rupert Brooke, saw Persia (present-day Iran) through the writings of Gertrude Bell and Vita Sackville-West, joined Charles Darwin on his exploration of Chile, and witnessed the former Yugoslavia through the eyes of Rebecca West.

The Writer Abroad takes the reader on a journey through history, often through countries which no longer exist, and recalls customs that have changed beyond recognition. It reveals the stories of huge cities, vast open landscapes and tiny remote villages in every continent of the globe. The experiences of visiting all of these places not only shaped the world of the intrepid travellers who wrote about them, but also shaped the vision and world perceptions of their readers.

Lucinda Hawksley

Africa

Democratic Republic of Congo

Joseph Conrad, *Congo Diary*, 1978

Saturday, 5th July [1890]

Today fell into a muddy puddle. Beastly. The fault of the man that carried me. After camp[in]g went to a small stream, bathed and washed clothes. Getting jolly well sick of this fun.

Tomorrow expect a long march to get to Nsona, 2 days from Manyanga. No sunshine today.

Monday, 7th July [1890]

Night miserably cold. No sleep. Mosquitoes.

Tuesday 29th [July 1890]

Today did not set the tent but put up in Govt shimbek. Zanzibari in charge – very obliging. Met ripe pineapple for the first time. On the road today passed a skeleton tied up to a post. Also white man's grave – no name. Heap of stones in the form of a cross.

EGYPT

Harriet Martineau, *Eastern Life, Present and Past*, 1848

At ten o'clock, one morning, Mrs. Y. and I were home from our early ride, and dressed for our visit to a hareem of a high order.

The lady to whose kindness we mainly owed this opportunity, accompanied us, with her daughter. We had a disagreeable drive in the carriage belonging to the hotel, knocking against asses, horses and people all the way. We alighted at the entrance of a paved passage leading to a court which we crossed: and then, in a second court, we were before the entrance of the hareem.

A party of eunuchs stood before a faded curtain, which they held aside when the gentlemen of our party and the dragoman had gone forward. Retired some way behind the curtain stood, in a half circle, eight or ten slave girls, in an attitude of deep obeisance. Two of them then took charge of each of us, holding us by the arms above the elbows, to help us up stairs. – After crossing a lobby at the top of the stairs, we entered a handsome apartment, where lay the chief wife, – at that time an invalid. – The ceiling was gayly painted; and so were the walls, – the latter with curiously bad attempts at domestic perspective. There were four handsome mirrors; and the curtains in the doorway were of a beautiful shawl fabric, fringed and tasseled. A Turkey carpet not only covered the whole floor, but was turned up at the corners. Deewans extended round nearly the whole room, – a lower one for ordinary use, and a high one for the seat of honor. The windows, which had a sufficient fence of blinds, looked upon a pretty garden, where I saw orange trees and many others, and the fences were hung with rich creepers.

On cushions on the floor lay the chief lady, ill and miserable-looking. She rose as we entered; but we made her lie down again: and she was then covered with a silk counterpane. Her dress was, as we saw when she rose, loose trowsers of blue striped cotton under her black silk jacket; and the same blue cotton appeared at the wrists, under her black sleeves. Her head-dress was of black net, bunched out curiously behind. Her hair was braided down the sides of this head-dress behind, and the ends were pinned over her forehead.

Lucie Duff Gordon, *Letters from Egypt*, 1861

Our procession home to the boat was very droll. *Mme*. Mounier could not ride an Arab saddle, so I lent her mine and *enfourche'd* my donkey, and away we went with men running with 'meshhaals' (fire-baskets on long poles) and lanterns, and the captain shouting out 'Full speed!' and such English phrases all the way – like a regular old salt as he is. We got here last night, and this morning Mustapha A'gha and the Nazir came down to conduct me up to my palace. I have such a big rambling house all over the top of the temple of Khem. How I wish I had you and the chicks to fill it! We had about twenty *fellahs* to clean the dust of *three years'* accumulation, and my room looks quite handsome with carpets and a divan. Mustapha's little girl found her way here when she heard I was come, and it seemed quite pleasant to have her playing on the carpet with a dolly and some sugar-plums, and making a feast for dolly on a saucer, arranging the sugar-plums Arab fashion.

She was monstrously pleased with Rainie's picture and kissed it. Such a quiet, nice little brown tot, and curiously like Rainie and walnut-juice.

The view all round my house is magnificent on every side, over the Nile in front facing north-west, and over a splendid range of green and distant orange buff hills to the south-east, where I have a spacious covered terrace. It is rough and dusty to the extreme, but will be very pleasant. Mustapha came in just now to offer me the loan of a horse, and to ask me to go to the mosque in a few nights to see the illumination in honour of a great Sheykh, a son of Sidi Hosseyn or Hassan. I asked whether my presence might not offend any Muslimeen, and he would not hear of such a thing. The sun set while he was here, and he asked if I objected to his praying in my presence, and went through his four *rekahs* very comfortably on my carpet. My next-door neighbour (across the courtyard all filled with antiquities) is a nice little Copt who looks like an antique statue himself. I shall *voisiner* with his family. He sent me coffee as soon as I arrived, and came to help. I am invited to El-Moutaneh, a few hours up the river, to visit the Mouniers, and to Keneh to visit Seyyid Achmet, and also the head of the merchants there who settled the price of a carpet for me in the bazaar, and seemed to like me. He was just one of those handsome, high-bred, elderly merchants with whom a story always begins in the Arabian Nights. When I can talk I will go and see a real Arab hareem. A very nice English couple, a man and his wife, gave me breakfast in their boat, and turned out to be business connections of Ross's, of the name of Arrowsmith; they were going to Assouan, and I shall see them on their way back. I asked Mustapha about the Arab young lady, and he spoke very highly of her, and is to let me know if she comes here and to offer hospitality from me: he did not know her name – she is called 'el *Haggeh*' (the Pilgrimess).

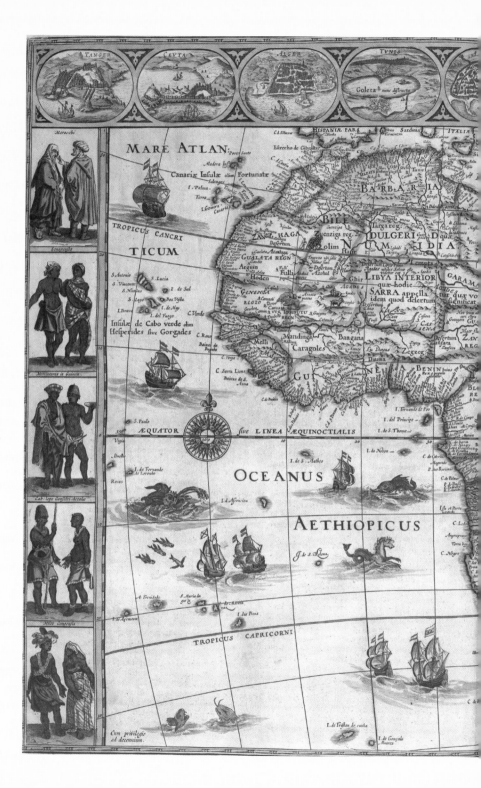

TANGER   CEVTA   ALGER   TVNIS

Goleta nunc distructa

Marocchi

Senegenses

Mercatores in Guinea

Cabi lopo Gonſalvi Accolæ

Nitei Conacuſta

MARE ATLAN:

TROPICUS CANCRI
TICUM

Canariæ Insulæ olim Fortunatæ

S. Antonie   S. Lucia
S. Vincente
S. Nicolao   I. de Sal
S. Iago   Boa Viſta
I. Bravo   I. de May
   I. del Fuego   C. Verde

Insulæ de Cabo verde olim
Hesperides ſive Gorgades

HISPANIÆ PARS

BARBARIA

BILE
ZANHAGA   Zuenzigs reg.
N U M I D I A
olim   DULGERI D quæ
GUALATA REGN
Arguin
Hoden

LIBYA INTERIOR
quæ hodie
SARRA appella
idem quod deſertum

GENEHOA
REGIO

Mandinga   Bangana
Melli   Caragoles   La Dauas
   Dauma   Zegzeg

GUINE   BENIN

C. Rox
Baixas de
Bugula
C. Verga
C. Serra Liona
Baixas de S.
Anna
C. de Baixos

ÆQUATOR   ſive LINEA ÆQUINOCTIALIS

OCEANUS

AETHIOPICUS

I. de S. Matheo
I. de Nobon
I. Aſcenſion

J. de S. Helena

A. Trinidad   S. Maria da
gor   As. Arena
I. dos Picos

TROPICUS CAPRICORNI

I. de Triſtan de cunha
I. de Gonçalo
Alvares

Cum privilegio
ad decennium.

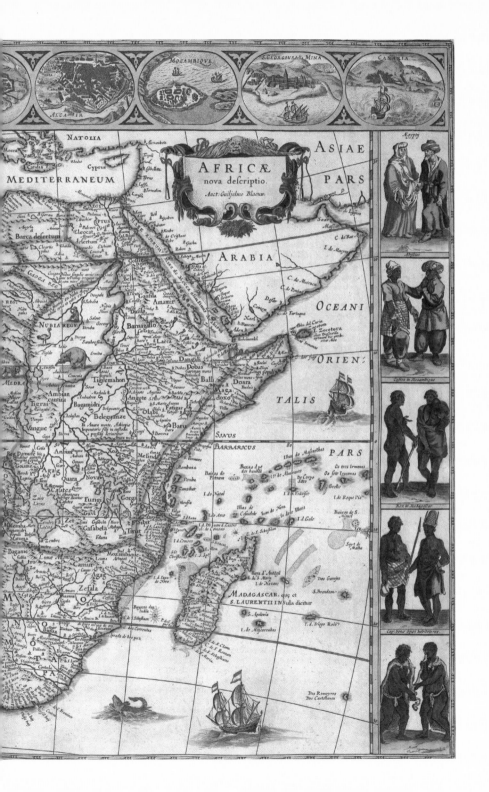

ALCAIR · MOZAMBIQVE · S. GEORGIVS della MINA · CANARIA

AFRICÆ
nova descriptio.
Auct: Guilielmo Blaeuw.

NATOLIA · ASIAE PARS

MEDITERRANEUM · Cyprus

ARABIA

OCEANI

ORIEN:

TALIS

Barca desertum

NUBIA REGN

GAOGA REG

REG

MEDRA

Tigremahon

Bagamidri

Beleguanze

Vangue

Ambian cantica

SINVS

BARBARICVS

PARS

MELINDA

Mombaza

Zanzibar

Quiloa

I. de Natal

Baxas do Padram

I. de S. Laurenzo

Ilhas de Comoro

MADAGASCAR, quæ et
S. LAURENTII INSULA dicitur

S. Apolonia

I. de Majcarenhas

I. A. Diego Roiz

Dos Romeyros
Dos Castelhanes

MOOMTAPA

Zefala

Agyptii

Abissini

Cafres in Mozambique

Rex in Madagascar

Cap. bone Spei habitatores

Thursday – Now I am settled in my Theban palace, it seems more and more beautiful, and I am quite melancholy that you cannot be here to enjoy it. The house is very large and has good thick walls, the comfort of which we feel to-day for it blows a hurricane; but indoors it is not at all cold. I have glass windows and doors to some of the rooms. It is a lovely dwelling. Two funny little owls as big as my fist live in the wall under my window, and come up and peep in, walking on tip-toe, and looking inquisitive like the owls in the hieroglyphics; and a splendid horus (the sacred hawk) frequents my lofty balcony. Another of my contemplar gods I sacrilegiously killed last night, a whip snake.

E.M. Forster, *Alexandria: A History and a Guide*, 1922

The Greco-Roman Museum

This collection was not formed until 1891, by which time, most of the antiquities in the neighbourhood had passed into private hands. It is consequently not of the first order and little in it has outstanding beauty. Used rightly, it is of great value, but the visitor who 'goes through' it will find afterwards that it has gone through him, and that he is left with nothing but a vague memory of fatigue.

* * *

Having returned as far as Ras-el-Tin Palace, we bear to the left, and follow the tram line along the shore of Anfouchi Bay. The Bay is very shallow and the entrance is protected by reefs. Pirates used it once. Native boat builders work along its beach and are pleasant to watch. In the corner is Anfouchi Pier, with a bathing establishment; beyond, on a small promontory, stands all that is left of Fort Adda; Arabi had his powder stored here in 1882, and the English blew it up. Now the tram turns a sharp corner, and a second Fort swings into view – Fort Kait Bey.

Fort Kait Bey (The 'Pharos')

This battered and neglected little peninsula is perhaps the most interesting spot in Alexandria, for here, rising to an incredible height, once stood the Pharos Lighthouse, the wonder of the world.

* * *

And now let the visitor (if the effort is not beyond him) elevate himself 400 feet higher into the air. Let him replace the Ras-el-Tin lighthouse to a temple to Poseidon; let him delete the mosques and the ground they stand on, and imagine in their place an expanse of water crossed by a Dyke; let him add to 'Pompey's Pillar' the Temple of Serapis and Isis and the vast buttressed walls of the library; let him turn Kom-al-Dik into a gorgeous and fantastic park, with the Tomb of Alexander at its feet; and the Eastern suburbs into gardens; and finally let him suppose that it is not Silsileh that stretches towards him but the peak of the Ptolemaic Palace, sheltering to its right the ships of the royal fleet and flanked on the landward side by the tiers of the theatre and the groves of the Mouseion. – Then he may have some conception of what Ancient Alexandria looked like from the summit of the Pharos – what she looked like when the Arabs entered in the autumn of 641.

The tram now follows the curve of the Eastern Harbour, a beautifully shaped basin. It was the main harbour of the ancients, but Mohammed Ali when he planned the modern city, developed the Western instead. There is a sea wall in two stages, to break the waves which dash right on to the road in rough weather; and there is a very fine promenade – the New Quays – which stretches all the way from Kait Bey to Silsileh. A walk along it can be delightful, though occasionally marred by bad smells. – We pass, right, the Bouseiri Mosque (see above) and finally come to the French Gardens, that connect with the Square, whence we started.

Leigh Hunt, 'A Thought of the Nile', 1818

It flows through old hushed Egypt and its sands,
Like some grave mighty thought threading a dream,
And times and things, as in that vision, seem
Keeping along it their eternal stands, –
Caves, pillars, pyramids, the shepherd bands
That roamed through the young world, the glory extreme
Of high Sesostris, and that southern beam,
The laughing queen that caught the world's great hands.

Then comes a mightier silence, stern and strong,
As of a world left empty of its throng,
And the void weighs on us; and then we wake,
And hear the fruitful stream lapsing along
Twixt villages, and think how we shall take
Our own calm journey on for human sake.

ETHIOPIA

James Bruce, *Travels between the Years 1768 and 1773…*, 1790

In the capital, where one is safe from surprise at all times, or in the country or villages, when the rains have become so constant that the valleys will not bear a horse to pass them, or that men cannot venture far from home through fear of being surrounded and swept away by temporary torrents, occasioned by sudden showers on the mountains; in a word, when a man can say he is safe at home, and the spear and shield are hung up in the hall, a number of people of the best fashion in the villages, of both sexes, courtiers in the palace, or citizens in the town, meet together to dine between twelve and one o'clock.

A long table is set in the middle of a large room, and benches beside it for a number of guests who are invited. Tables and

benches the Portuguese introduced amongst them; but bull hides, spread upon the ground, served them before, as they do in the camp and country now.

Sir Richard Burton, *Wanderings in Three Continents*, 1901

The country now became romantic and beautiful – a confusion of lofty stony mountains, plantations of the finest coffee, scatters of villages, forests of noble trees, with rivulets of the coolest and clearest water. We here stood some five thousand five hundred feet high, and although only nine degrees removed from the Line, the air was light and pleasant. It made me remember the climate of Aden, and hate it.

We slept en route, and on January 3rd we first sighted Harar City. On the crest of a hill distant two miles it appeared, a long sombre line strikingly contrasting with the whitewashed settlements of the more civilised East, and nothing broke the outline except the two grey and rudely shaped minarets of the Jami, or Maritz (cathedral).

MOROCCO

George Orwell, *Marrakech*, 1939

As the corpse went past the flies left the restaurant table in a cloud and rushed after it, but they came back a few minutes later.

The little crowd of mourners-all men and boys, no women – threaded their way across the market-place between the piles of pomegranates and the taxis and the camels, wailing a short chant over and over again. What really appeals to the flies is that the corpses here are never put into coffins, they are merely wrapped in a piece of rag and carried on a rough wooden bier on the shoulders of four friends. When the friends get to the burying-ground they hack an oblong hole a foot or two deep, dump the body in it and fling over it a little of the dried-up, lumpy earth, which is like broken brick. No gravestone, no name, no identifying mark of any kind. The burying-ground is merely a huge waste of hummocky earth, like a derelict building-lot. After a month or two no one can even be certain where his own relatives are buried.

When you walk through a town like this – two hundred thousand inhabitants, of whom at least twenty thousand own literally nothing except the rags they stand up in – when you see how the people live, and still more how easily they die, it is always difficult to believe that you are walking among human beings. All colonial empires are in reality founded upon that fact. The people have brown faces – besides, there are so many of them! Are they really the same flesh as yourself? Do they even have names? Or are they merely a kind of undifferentiated brown stuff, about as individual as bees or coral insects? They rise out of the earth, they sweat and starve for a few years, and then they sink back into the nameless mounds of the graveyard and nobody notices that they are gone. And even the graves themselves soon fade back into the soil. Sometimes, out for a walk, as you break your way through the prickly pear, you notice that it is rather bumpy underfoot, and only a certain regularity in the bumps tells you that you are walking over skeletons.

I was feeding one of the gazelles in the public gardens.

Gazelles are almost the only animals that look good to eat when they are still alive, in fact, one can hardly look at their hindquarters without thinking of mint sauce. The gazelle I was feeding seemed to know that this thought was in my mind, for though it took the piece of bread I was holding out it obviously did not like me. It nibbled rapidly at the bread, then lowered its head and tried to butt me, then took another nibble and then butted again. Probably its idea was that if it could drive me away the bread would somehow remain hanging in mid-air

An Arab navvy working on the path nearby lowered his heavy hoe and sidled towards us. He looked from the gazelle to the bread and from the bread to the gazelle, with a sort of quiet amazement, as though he had never seen anything quite like this before. Finally he said shyly in French:

'*I* could eat some of that bread.'

I tore off a piece and he stowed it gratefully in some secret place under his rags. This man is an employee of the Municipality.

When you go through the Jewish quarters you gather some idea of what the medieval ghettoes were probably like. Under their Moorish rulers the Jews were only allowed to own land in certain restricted areas, and after centuries of this kind of treatment they have ceased to bother about overcrowding. Many of the streets are a good deal less than six feet wide, the houses are completely windowless, and sore-eyed children cluster everywhere in unbelievable numbers, like clouds of flies. Down the centre of the street there is generally running a little river of urine.

In the bazaar huge families of Jews, all dressed in the long black robe and little black skull-cap, are working in dark fly-infested booths that look like caves. A carpenter sits cross-legged at a prehistoric lathe, turning chair-legs at lightning speed. He works the lathe with a bow in his right hand and guides the chisel with his left foot, and thanks to a lifetime of sitting in this position his left leg is warped out of shape. At his side his grandson, aged six, is already starting on the simpler parts of the job.

I was just passing the coppersmiths' booths when somebody noticed that I was lighting a cigarette. Instantly, from the dark holes all round, there was a frenzied rush of Jews, many of them old grandfathers with flowing grey beards, all clamouring for a cigarette. Even a blind man somewhere at the back of one of the booths heard a rumour of cigarettes and came crawling out, groping in the air with his hand. In about a minute I had used up the whole packet. None of these people, I suppose, works less than twelve hours a day, and every one of them looks on a cigarette as a more or less impossible luxury.

As the Jews live in self-contained communities they follow the same trades as the Arabs, except for agriculture. Fruit-sellers, potters, silversmiths, blacksmiths, butchers, leather-workers, tailors, water-carriers, beggars, porters – whichever way you look you see nothing but Jews. As a matter of fact there are thirteen thousand of them, all living in the space of a few acres. A good job Hitler isn't here. Perhaps he is on his way, however. You hear the usual dark rumours about the Jews, not only from the Arabs but from the poorer Europeans.

'Yes, *mon vieux*, they took my job away from me and gave it to a Jew. The Jews! They're the real rulers of this country, you know. They've got all the money. They control the banks, finance – everything.'

'But,' I said, 'isn't it a fact that the average Jew is a labourer working for about a penny an hour?'

'Ah, that's only for show! They're all money-lenders really. They're cunning, the Jews.'

In just the same way, a couple of hundred years ago, poor old women used to be burned for witchcraft when they could not even work enough magic to get themselves a square meal.

All people who work with their hands are partly invisible, and the more important the work they do, the less visible they are. Still, a white skin is always fairly conspicuous. In northern Europe, when you see a labourer ploughing a field, you probably give him a second glance. In a hot country, anywhere south of Gibraltar or east of Suez, the chances are that you don't even see him. I have noticed this again and again. In a tropical landscape one's eye takes in everything except the human beings. It takes in the dried-up soil, the prickly pear, the palm-tree and the distant mountain, but it always misses the peasant hoeing at his patch. He is the same colour as the earth, and a great deal less interesting to look at.

It is only because of this that the starved countries of Asia and Africa are accepted as tourist resorts. No one would think of running cheap trips to the Distressed Areas. But where the human beings have brown skins their poverty is simply not noticed. What does Morocco mean to a Frenchman? An orange-grove or a job in government service. Or to an Englishman? Camels, castles, palm-trees, Foreign Legionnaires, brass trays and bandits. One could probably live here for years without noticing that for nine-tenths of the people the reality of life is an endless, back-breaking struggle to wring a little food out of an eroded soil.

Most of Morocco is so desolate that no wild animal bigger than a hare can live on it. Huge areas which were once covered with forest have turned into a treeless waste where the soil is exactly like broken-up brick. Nevertheless a good deal of it is cultivated, with frightful labour. Everything is done by hand. Long lines of women, bent double like inverted capital Ls, work their way slowly across the fields, tearing up the prickly weeds with their hands, and the peasant gathering lucerne for fodder pulls it up stalk by stalk instead of reaping it, thus saving an inch or two on each stalk. The plough is a wretched wooden thing, so frail that one can easily carry it on one's shoulder, and fitted underneath with a rough iron spike which stirs the soil to a depth of about four inches. This is as much as the strength of the animals is equal to. It is usual to plough with a cow and a donkey yoked together. Two donkeys would not be quite strong enough, but on the other hand two cows would cost a little more to feed. The peasants possess no harrows, they merely plough the soil several times over in different directions, finally leaving it in rough furrows, after which the whole field has to be shaped with hoes into small oblong patches, to conserve water. Except for a day or two after the rare rainstorms there is never enough water. Along the edges of the fields channels are hacked out to a depth of thirty or forty feet to get at the tiny trickles which run through the subsoil.

Every afternoon a file of very old women passes down the road outside my house, each carrying a load of firewood. All of them are mummified with age and the sun, and all of them are tiny. It seems to be generally the case in primitive communities that the women, when they get beyond a certain age, shrink to the size of children. One day a poor old creature who could not have been more than four feet tall crept past me under a vast load of wood. I stopped her and put a five-sou piece (a little more than a farthing) into her hand. She answered with a shrill wail, almost a scream, which was partly gratitude but mainly surprise. I suppose that from her point of view, by taking any notice of her, I seemed almost to be violating a law of nature. She accepted her status as an old woman, that is to say as a beast of burden. When a family is travelling it is quite usual to see a father and a grown-up son riding ahead on donkeys, and an old woman following on foot, carrying the baggage.

But what is strange about these people is their invisibility. For several weeks, always at about the same time of day, the file of old women had hobbled past the house with their firewood, and though they had registered themselves on my eyeballs I cannot truly say that I had seen them. Firewood was passing – that was how I saw it. It was only that one day I happened to be walking behind them, and the curious up-and-down motion of a load of wood drew my attention to the human being underneath it. Then for the first time I noticed the poor old earth-coloured bodies, bodies reduced to bones and leathery skin, bent double under the crushing weight. Yet I suppose I had not been five minutes on Moroccan soil before I noticed the overloading of the donkeys and was infuriated by it. There is no question that the donkeys are damnably treated. The Moroccan donkey is hardly bigger than a St Bernard dog, it carries a load which in the British army would be considered too much for a fifteen-hands mule, and very often its pack-saddle is not taken off its back for weeks together.

But what is peculiarly pitiful is that it is the most willing creature on earth, it follows its master like a dog and does not need either bridle or halter. After a dozen years of devoted work it suddenly drops dead, whereupon its master tips it into the ditch and the village dogs have torn its guts out before it is cold.

This kind of thing makes one's blood boil, whereas – on the whole – the plight of the human beings does not. I am not commenting, merely pointing to a fact. People with brown skins are next door to invisible. Anyone can be sorry for the donkey with its galled back, but it is generally owing to some kind of accident if one even notices the old woman under her load of sticks.

As the storks flew northward the Negroes were marching southward – a long, dusty column, infantry, screw-gun batteries and then more infantry, four or five thousand men in all, winding up the road with a clumping of boots and a clatter of iron wheels.

They were Senegalese, the blackest Negroes in Africa, so black that sometimes it is difficult to see whereabouts on their necks the hair begins. Their splendid bodies were hidden in reach-me-down khaki uniforms, their feet squashed into boots that looked like blocks of wood, and every tin hat seemed to be a couple of sizes too small. It was very hot and the men had marched a long way. They slumped under the weight of their packs and the curiously sensitive black faces were glistening with sweat.

As they went past a tall, very young Negro turned and caught my eye. But the look he gave me was not in the least the kind of look you might expect. Not hostile, not contemptuous, not sullen, not even inquisitive. It was the shy, wide-eyed Negro look, which actually is a look of profound respect. I saw how it was. This wretched boy, who is a French citizen and has therefore been dragged from the forest to scrub floors and catch syphilis in garrison towns, actually has feelings of reverence before a white skin. He has been taught that the white race are his masters, and he still believes it.

But there is one thought which every white man (and in this connection it doesn't matter twopence if he calls himself a Socialist) thinks when he sees a black army marching past. 'How much longer can we go on kidding these people? How long before they turn their guns in the other direction?'

It was curious, really. Every white man there has this thought stowed somewhere or other in his mind. I had it, so had the other onlookers, so had the officers on their sweating chargers and the white NCOs marching in the ranks. It was a kind of secret which we all knew and were too clever to tell; only the Negroes didn't know it. And really it was almost like watching a flock of cattle to see the long column, a mile or two miles of armed men, flowing peacefully up the road, while the great white birds drifted over them in the opposite direction, glittering like scraps of paper.

1939

NIGERIA

Sir Richard Burton, *Abeokuta and the Camaroons Mountains: An Exploration*, 1863

The first aspect of Abeokuta was decidedly remarkable. The principal peculiarity was the fantastic breaking of the undulating plain by masses of grey granite – the rose-coloured is not easily seen – between twenty and thirty in number, sometimes rising two hundred and fifty to three hundred feet above the lower levels. White under the sun's glare, and cast in strange forms – knobs, pinnacles, walls, backbones, scarps, and logans – they towered over the patches of dark trees at their bases and the large brown villages, or rather towns, which separated them. There was a long dorsum, which nearly bisected the town from north to south, and which lay like a turtle's back between the scattered lines of habitations.

SOMALIA

Sir Richard Burton, *Wanderings in Three Continents*, 1901

I was delayed twenty-seven days whilst a route was debated upon, mules were sent for, camels were bought, and an abban, or protector-guide, was secured. Hereabouts no stranger could travel without such a patron, who was paid to defend his client's life and property. Practically he took his money and ran away. On the evening of November 27th, 1864, the caravan was ready. It consisted of five camels laden with provisions, cooking-pots, ammunition, and our money–that is to say, heads, coarse tobacco, American sheeting, Indian cotton, and indigo-dyed stuffs. The escort was formed by the two policemen, the 'End of Time,' and Yusuf, a one-eyed lad from Zayla, with the guide and his tail of three followers. My men were the pink of Somali fashion. They had stained their hair of a light straw colour by plastering it with ashes; they had teased it till it stood up a full foot, and they had mutually spirted upon their wigs melted tallow, making their heads look like giant cauliflowers that contrasted curiously with the bistre-coloured skins. Their Tobes (togas) were dazzlingly white, with borders dazzlingly red. Outside the dress was strapped a horn-hiked two-edged dagger, long and heavy; their 34 shields of rhinoceros hide were brand new, and their two spears poised upon the right shoulder were freshly scraped and oiled, and blackened and polished. They had added my spare rifle and guns to the camel loads–the things were well enough in Aden, but in Somali we would deride such strange, unmanly weapons. They balanced themselves upon dwarf Abyssinian saddles, extending the leg and raising the heel like the haute ecolé of Louis XIV. The stirrup was an iron ring admitting only the big toe, and worse than that of the Sertanejo. As usual in this country, where the gender masculine will not work, we had two cooks – tall, buxom, muscular dames, chocolate skinned and round faced. They had curiously soft and fluted voices, hardly to be expected from their square and huge-hipped figures, and contrasting agreeably with the harsh organs of the men. Their feet were bare, their veil was confined by a narrow fillet, and the body-cloth was an indigo-dyed cotton, girt at the waist and graceful as a winding sheet. I never saw them eat; probably, as the people say of cooks, they lived by sucking their fingers.

TANZANIA

Sir Richard Burton, *Wanderings in Three Continents*, 1901

The next day we sighted the plateau of Ugogo and its eastern desert. The spectacle was truly impressive. The first aspect was stern and wild – the rough nurse of rugged men. We went on the descent from day to day until September 18th, when a final march of four hours placed us on the plains of Ugogo. Before noon I sighted from a sharp turn in the bed of a river our tent pitched

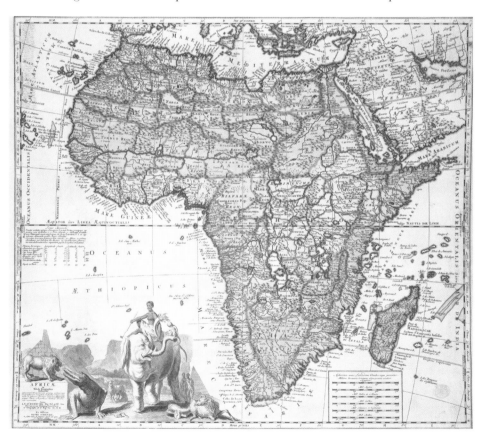

under a huge sycamore, on a level step. It was a pretty spot in the barren scene, grassy, and grown with green mimosas, and here we halted for a while. The second stage of our journey was accomplished. After three days' sojourn at Ugogo to recruit the party and lay in rations for four long desert marches, we set forth on our long march through the province of Ugogo. Our first day's journey was over a grassy country, and we accomplished it in comparative comfort. The next day we toiled through the sunshine of the hot waste, crossing plains over paths where the slides of elephants' feet upon the last year's muddy clay showed that the land was not always dry. During this journey we suffered many discomforts and difficulties. The orb of day glowed like a fireball in our faces; then our path would take us through dense, thorny jungle, and over plains of black, cracked earth. Our caravan once rested in a thorny copse based upon rich red and yellow clay; once it was hurriedly dislodged by a swarm of wild bees, and the next morning I learnt that we had sustained a loss – one of our porters had deserted, and to his care had been committed one of the most valuable of our packages, a portmanteau containing 'The Nautical Almanac,' surveying books, and most of our papers, pen, and ink.

* * *

When we resumed our journey, the heat was awful. The sun burnt like the breath of a bonfire, warm siroccos raised clouds of dust, and in front of us the horizon was so distant that, as the Arabs expressed themselves, a man might be seen three marches off.

Roald Dahl, *Going Solo*, 1986

When I woke up the next morning the ship's engines had stopped. I jumped out of my bunk and peered through the port-hole. This was my first glimpse of Dar es Salaam and I have never forgotten it. We were anchored out in the middle of a vast rippling blue-black lagoon and all around the rim of the lagoon there were pale-yellow sandy beaches, almost white, and breakers were running up on to the sand, and coconut palms with their little green leafy hats were growing on the beaches, and there were casuarina trees, immensely tall and breathtakingly beautiful with their delicate grey-green foliage. And then behind the casuarinas was what seemed to me like a jungle, a great tangle of tremendous dark-green trees that were full of shadows and almost certainly teeming, so I told myself, with rhinos and lions and all manner of vicious beasts. Over to one side lay the tiny town of Dar es Salaam, the houses white and yellow and pink, and among the houses I could see a narrow church steeple and a domed mosque and along the waterfront there was a line of acacia trees splashed with scarlet flowers. A fleet of canoes was rowing out to take us ashore and the black-skinned rowers were chanting weird songs in time with their rowing.

Only once did I see any elephant. I saw a big tusker and his cow and their one baby moving slowly forward in line astern about fifty yards from the road on the edge of the forest. I stopped the car to watch them but I did not get out. The elephants never saw me and I was able to stay gazing at them for quite a while. A great sense of peace and serenity seemed to surround these massive, slow-moving, gentle beasts. Their skin hung loose over their bodies like suits they had inherited from larger ancestors, with the trousers ridiculously baggy. Like the giraffes they were vegetarians and did not have to hunt or kill in order to survive in the jungle, and no other wild beast would ever dare to threaten them. Only the foul humans in the shape of an occasional big-game hunter or an ivory poacher were to be feared, but this small elephant family did not look as though they had yet met any of these horrors. They seemed to be leading a life of absolute contentment. They are better off than me, I told myself, and a good deal wiser. I myself am at this moment on my way to kill Germans or to be killed by them, but those elephants have no thought of murder in their minds.

TUNISIA

Aldous Huxley, *In a Tunisian Oasis*, 1925

At Tozeur, when at last we arrived, it had just finished raining – for the first time in two and a half years – and now the wind had sprung up: there was a sandstorm. A thick brown fog, whirled into eddies by the wind, gritty to the skin, abolished the landscape from before our smarting eyes. We sneezed: there was sand in our ears, in our hair, between our teeth. It was horrible. I felt depressed, but not surprised. The weather is always horrible when I travel. Once, in a French hotel, I was accused of having brought with me the flat black bugs, of whose presence among my bed-clothes I complained to a self-righteous proprietress. I defended myself with energy against the impeachment. Bugs – no: I am innocent of bugs. But when it comes to bad weather I have to plead guilty. Rain, frost, wind, snow, hail, fog – I bring them with me wherever I go. I bring them to places where they have never been heard of, at seasons when it is impossible that they should occur. What delightful skating there will be in the Spice Islands when we arrive! On this particular journey I had brought with me to every place on my itinerary the most appalling meteorological calamities. At Naples, for example, it was the snow. Coming out of the theatre on the night of our arrival, we found it lying an inch deep under the palm trees in the public gardens. And Vesuvius, next morning, glittered white, like Fujiyama, against the pale spring sky. At Palermo there was a cloudburst. 'Between the Syrtes and soft Sicily' we passed through a tempest of hail, lightening, and wind. At Tunis it very nearly froze. At Sousse the wind was so violent that the stiff boardlike leaves of the cactuses swayed and trembled in the air like aspens. And now on the day of our arrival at Tozeur, it had rained for the first time in thirty months, and there was a sandstorm. No I was not in the least surprised; but I could not help feeling a little gloomy. Toward evening the wind somewhat abated; the sand began to drop out of the air. At midday the brown curtain had been impenetrable at fifty yards. It thinned, grew gauzier; one could see objects at a hundred, two hundred yards. From the windows of the hotel bedroom in which we had sat all day, trying – but in vain, for it came through even invisible crannies – to escape from the wind-blown sand, we could see the fringes of a dense forest of palm trees, the dome of a little mosque, houses of sun-dried brick, and thin brown men in flapping nightshirts walking, with muffled faces and bent heads, against the wind, or riding, sometimes astride, sometimes sideways, on the bony rumps of patient little asses. Two professional tourists in sun helmets – there was no sun – emerged round the corner of a street. A malicious gust of wind caught them unawares; simultaneously the two helmets shot into the air, thudded, rolled in the dust. The two professional tourists scuttled in pursuit. The spectacle cheered us a little; we descended, we ventured out of doors.

LIBYA

Roald Dahl, *Going Solo*, 1986

I flew straight for the point where the Squadron airfield should have been. It wasn't there. I flew around the area to north, south, east and west, but there was not a sign of an airfield. Below me there was nothing but empty desert, and rather rugged desert at that, full of large stones and boulders and gullies.

At this point, dusk began to fall and I realized that I was in trouble. My fuel was running low and there was no way I could get back to Fouka on what I had left. I couldn't have found it in the dark anyway. The only course open to me now was to make a forced landing in the desert and make it quickly, before it was too dark to see.

I skimmed low over the boulder-strewn desert searching for just one small strip of reasonably flat sand on which to land. I knew the direction of the wind so I knew precisely the direction that my approach should take. But where, oh where was there one little patch of desert that was clear of boulders and gullies and lumps of rock. There simply wasn't one. It was nearly dark now. I had to get down somehow or other. I chose a piece of ground that seemed to me to be as boulder-free as any and I made an approach. I came in as slowly as I dared, hanging on the prop, travelling just above my stalling speed of eighty miles an hour. My wheels touched down. I throttled back and prayed for a bit of luck.

I didn't get it. My undercarriage hit a boulder and collapsed completely and the Gladiator buried its nose in the sand at what must have been about seventy-five miles an hour.

Middle East

IRAN / PERSIA

Vita Sackville-West, *Passenger to Teheran*, 1926

We met little donkeys, coming down, stepping delicately, and camels, swaying down on their soft padded feet. Looking up, we could see the whole road of the pass zigzagging up the cliff-side, populous with animals and shouting, thrashing men. Looking back, as we climbed, we could see the immense prospect of the plain stretching away behind us. A savage, desolating country! But one that filled me with extraordinary elation. I had never seen anything that pleased me so well as these Persian uplands, with their enormous views, clear light, and rocky grandeur. This was, in detail, in actuality, the region labelled 'Persia' on the maps. Let me be aware, I said; let me savour every mile of the way. But there were too many miles, and although I gazed, sitting in the front seat, the warm body of the dog pressed against me, the pungent smell of the sheepskin in my nostrils, it is only the general horizon that I remember, and not every unfolding of the way. This question of horizon, however; how important it is; how it alters the shape of the mind; how it expresses, essentially, one's ultimate sense of country! That is what can never be told in words: the exact size, proportion, contour; the new standard to which the mind must adjust itself.

Gertrude Bell, *The Letters of Gertrude Bell*, 1927

It's a corner so full of associations. So many times I've come over the Bagdad-Karbala road after long desert expeditions with a sense of accomplishment, and, at the same time, with that curious sense of disappointment which one nearly always feels with the accomplished thing. The best time, I think, was when I came back with the plan of Ukhaidir in my pocket – the worst when I came up from Arabia. I find myself forever stepping back into a former atmosphere – knowing with my real self that it has all melted away and yet half drugged with the lingering savour of it.

JORDAN

T.E. Lawrence, *Seven Pillars of Wisdom*, 1922

In the evening, when we had shut-to the gate, all guests would assemble, either in my room or in Ali's, and coffee and stories would go round until the last meal, and after it, till sleep came.

On stormy nights we brought in brushwood and dung and lit a great fire in the middle of the floor. About it would be drawn the carpets and the saddle-sheepskins, and in its light we would tell over our own battles, or hear the visitors' traditions. The leaping flames chased our smoke-muffled shadows strangely about the rough stone wall behind us, distorting them over the hollows and projections of its broken face. When these stories came to a period, our tight circle would shift over, uneasily, to the other knee or elbow; while coffee-cups went clinking round, and a servant fanned the blue reek of the fire towards the loophole with his cloak, making the glowing ash swirl and sparkle with his draught. Till the voice of the story-teller took up again, we would hear the rain-spots hissing briefly as they dripped from the stone-beamed roof into the fire's heart.

LEBANON

Herodotus, *The History of Herodotus*, 440 B.C.E

[Tyre in Phoenicia is in modern-day Lebanon]

I made a voyage to Tyre in Phoenicia, hearing there was a temple of Hercules at that place, very highly venerated. I visited the temple, and found it richly adorned with a number of offerings, among which two pillars, one of pure gold, were the other of emerald shining with great brilliancy at night. In a conversation which I held with the priests, I enquired how long their temple had been built, and found by their answer that they, too, differed from the Greeks. They said that the temple was built at the same time that the city was founded, and that the foundation of the city took place two thousand three hundred years ago. In Tyre I remarked another temple where the same god was worshipped as the Thasian Hercules. So I went on to Thasos, where I found temple of Hercules which had been built by the Phoenicians who

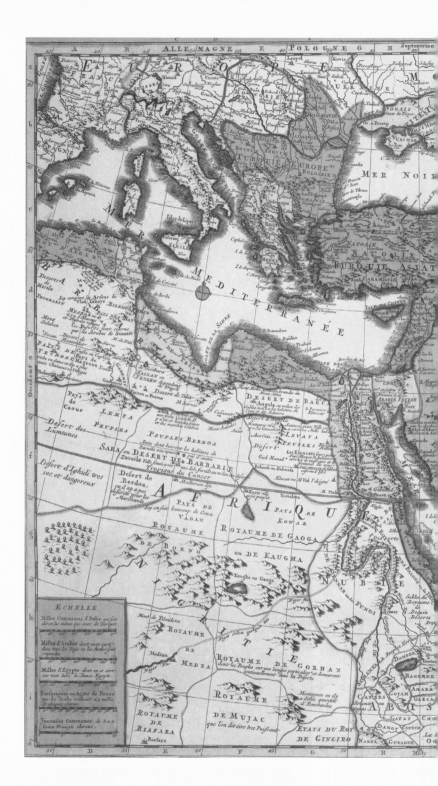

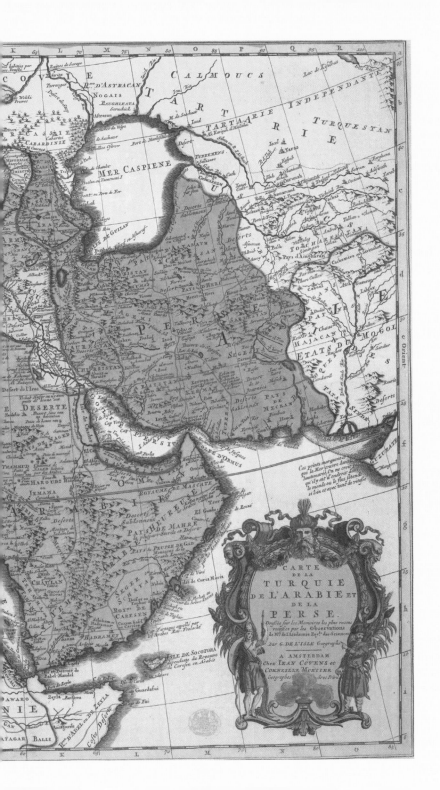

colonised that island when they sailed in search of Europa.' Even this was five generations earlier than the time when Hercules, son of Amphitryon, was born in Greece. These researches show plainly that there is an ancient god Hercules; and my own opinion is, that those Greeks act most wisely who build and maintain two temples of Hercules, in the one of which the Hercules worshipped is known by the name of Olympian, and has sacrifice offered to him as an immortal, while in the other, the honours paid are such as are due to a hero.

Ian Fleming, *Thrilling Cities*, 1963

An hour more of slow, spectacular sunset and blue-black night and then Beirut showed up ahead – a sprawl of twinkling hundreds-and-thousands under an Arabian Nights new moon that dived down into the oil lands as the Comet banked to make her landing.

Beirut is a crooked town and, when we came to rest, I advised my neighbour to leave nothing small on his seat, and particularly not his extremely expensive camera. I said that we were now entering the thieving areas of the world. Someone would get it. The hatch clanged open and the first sticky fingers of the East reached in. 'Our Man in the Lebanon' was there to meet me, full of the gossip of the bazaars. Beirut is the great smuggling junction of the world. Diamonds thieved from Sierra Leone come in here for onward passage to Germany, cigarettes and pornography from Tangier, arms for the sheikhs of Araby and drugs from Turkey.

SAUDI ARABIA

Sir Richard Burton, *Wanderings in Three Continents*, 1901

Yambu, the port of El Medinah, lies S.S.W. of, and a little over a hundred and thirty miles from, its city. The road was infamous– rocky, often waterless, alternately fiery and freezing, and infested with the Beni Harb, a villainous tribe of hill Bedouins. Their chief was one Saad, a brigand of the first water. He was described as a little brown man, contemptible in appearance but remarkable for courage and for a ready wit, which saved him from the poison and pistol of his enemies. Some called him the friend of the poor, and all knew him to be the foe of the rich.

There was nothing to see at Yambu, where, however, we enjoyed the hammam and the drinking-water, which appeared deliciously sweet after the briny supplies of Suez. By dint of abundant bargaining we hired camels at the moderate rate of three dollars each – half in ready money, the rest to be paid after arrival. I also bought a shugduf, or rude litter carrying two, and I chose the boy Mohammed as my companion. The journey is usually done in five days. We took eight, and we considered ourselves lucky fellows.

On the evening of the next day (July 18th) we set out with all the gravity of men putting our heads into the lion's jaws. The moon rose fair and clear as we emerged from the shadowy streets. When we launched into the desert, the sweet, crisp air delightfully contrasted with the close, offensive atmosphere of the town.

* * *

There are evidently eight degrees of pilgrims. The lowest walk, propped on heavy staves; these are the itinerant coffee-makers, sherbet sellers, and tobacconists, country folks driving flocks of sheep and goats with infinite clamour and gesticulation, negroes from distant Africa, and crowds of paupers, some approaching the supreme hour, but therefore yearning the more to breathe their last in the Holy City. Then come the humble riders of laden camels, mules, and asses, which the Bedouin, who clings baboon-like to the hairy back of his animal, despises, saying:–

Honourable to the rider is the riding of the horse;
But the mule is a dishonour, and a donkey a disgrace.

Respectable men mount dromedaries, or blood-camels, known by their small size, their fine limbs, and their large deer-like eyes: their saddles show crimson sheep-skins between tall metal pommels, and these are girthed over fine saddle-bags, whose long tassels of bright worsted hang almost to the ground. Irregular soldiers have picturesquely equipped steeds. Here and there rides some old Arab shaykh, preceded by his varlets performing a war-dance, compared with which the bear's performance is graceful, firing their duck-guns in the air, or blowing powder into the naked legs of those before them, brandishing their bared swords, leaping frantically with parti-coloured rags floating in the wind, and tossing high their long spears. Women, children, and invalids of the poorer classes sit upon rugs or carpets spread over the large boxes that form the camel's load. Those a little better off use a shibriyah, or short coat, fastened crosswise. The richer

prefer shugduf panniers with an awning like a miniature tent. Grandees have led horses and gorgeously painted takhtrawan – litters like the bangué of Brazil – borne between camels or mules with scarlet and brass trappings. The vehicle mainly regulates the pilgrim's expenses, which may vary from five pounds to as many thousands.

SYRIA

Sir Richard Burton, *Wanderings in Three Continents*, 1901

The beginning of the end is at the tenth and last station, El Hamah, meaning the Head of the Valley, and we halt here for a cup of coffee. The next place of note is Dummar; here we cross the Barada torrent. This place is, despite its low site and hot and cold air, a favourite for villas; and certain wealthy Damascus usurers have here built large piles, as remarkable for the barbarity of their outer frescoes as for the tawdry decoration of the interior. The witty Damasceines call them 'traps,' because they are periodically let to high officials for other considerations than hire. And now, with its slate-coloured stream, garnished with weirs on our right, the valley becomes broader and more important; the upper cliffs are tunnelled into cut caves, Troglodyte dwellings and sepulchres of the ancients; seven veins at high levels and at low levels branch off from the main artery; and, after passing a natural gateway formed by two shield-like masses of rock, we suspect that Damascus is before us.

The first sight of Damascus was once famous in travel. But then men rode on horseback, and turned, a little beyond Damascus, sharply to the left of the present line. They took what was evidently the old Roman road, and which is still, on account of its being a short cut, affected by muleteers. Now it is nothing but an ugly climb up sheet-rock and rolling stones, with bars and holes dug by the armed hoof of many a generation. They then passed through El Zaarub (the Spout); this is the old way, sunk some ten feet deep in the rock till it resembles an uncovered tunnel, and polished like glass by the traffic and transit of ages. At its mouth you suddenly turn a corner and see Damascus lying in panorama, a few hundred feet below you.

T. E. Lawrence's diary, 1911

[When he was writing, Syria also encompassed the land that is now Lebanon.]
Next day, Thursday: Up before sunrise, and out before feeding
for Ras el Ain 4 hours: stopped a little before and ate bread and
leben in Kurdish tent: chief more hospitable: gave him a hejub
to work at Tell Hamra if the English came: money refused. Went
on to Ras el Ain (½ hr.) and stayed there 1 ½ hrs. Drinking and
washing: very pleasant spot and good water. In afternoon walked
through liquorice and thick dust to Seruj. Took room at Khan and
enquired fruitlessly about camera: met Nouri Effendi. Rice and
Bahmia with bread. A little feverish.

Friday: Up and out for Urfa by carriage (1 med.) after giving ¼
to Khanji: slow drive: saw nothing: Urfa about mid-day (7 hrs.).
Took room in great Khan: then went out about 4 P.M. to photograph Castle. Took it from the due West showing the double gates
and the line of walls from the πυργοκάστελλος to the extreme end.
Warm, beautiful evening, with a little breeze. Rice and bahmia
with bread and was then kept awake half the night by a cheap
theatre in the café over the street. Police asked for my papers.

* * *

Tuesday, August: Up at sunrise after a fair night: dawn very
glorious, with the broken blacks of the foreground leading to
the silver line of the river, crossed by the rough points of the
near poplar trees, and then the hills beyond, from deepest black
at the water-edge, shaded to grey, purple, and finally a glorious
orange, as the light caught them. Sunrise of course poor, as most
sunrises are.

TURKEY

Lady Mary Wortley Montagu, *Embassy Letters*, 1716–18

I must not omit what I saw remarkable at Sofia, one of the most beautiful towns in the Turkish empire, and famous for its hot baths, that are resorted to both for diversion and health. I stopped here one day on purpose to see them. Designing to go incognito I hired a Turkish coach. These voitures are not at all like ours, but much more convenient for the country, the heat being so great that glasses would be very troublesome. They are made a good deal in the manner of the Dutch coaches, having wooden lattices painted and gilded, the inside being also painted with baskets and nosegays intermixed commonly with little poetical mottos. Covered all over with scarlet cloth, lined with silk, and very often richly embroidered and fringed. This covering entirely hides the persons in them, but may be thrown back at pleasure and the ladies peep through the lattices. They hold four people very conveniently, seated on cushions, but not raised.

In one of these covered waggons, I went to the bagnio about ten o'clock. It was already full of women. It is built of stone in the shape of a dome, with no windows but in the roof, which gives light enough. There was five of these domes joined together, the outmost being less than the rest and serving only as a hall, where the portress stood at the door. Ladies of quality generally give this woman the value of a crown or ten shillings and I did not forget that ceremony. The next room is a very large one paved with marble, and all round it raised two sofas of marble one above another. There were four fountains of cold water in this room, falling first into marble basins, and then running on the floor in little channels made for that purpose, which carried the streams into the next room, something less than this, with the same sort of marble sofas, but so hot with steams of sulphur proceeding from the baths joining to it, 'twas impossible to stay there with one's clothes on. The two other domes were the hot baths, one of which had cocks of cold water turning into it to temper it to what degree of warmth the bathers have a mind to.

I was in my travelling habit, which is a riding dress, and certainly appeared very extraordinary to them. Yet there was not one of them that showed the least surprise or impertinent curiosity, but received me with all the obliging civility possible. I know no European court where the ladies would have behaved themselves in so polite a manner to a stranger. I believe, in the whole, there were two hundred women, and yet none of those disdainful smiles or satirical whispers that never fail in our assemblies when anybody appears that is not dressed exactly in fashion. They repeated over and over to me; 'Güzelle, pek güzelle', which is nothing but

'charming, very charming'. The first sofas were covered with cushions and rich carpets, on which sat the ladies, and on the second their slaves behind them, but without any distinction of rank by their dress, all being in the state of nature, that is, in plain English, stark naked, without any beauty or defect concealed. Yet there was not the least wanton smile or immodest gesture amongst them. They walked and moved with the same majestic grace which Milton describes of our general mother. There were many amongst them as exactly proportioned as ever any goddess was drawn by the pencil of Guido or Titian, and most of their skins shiningly white, only adorned by their beautiful hair divided into many tresses, hanging on their shoulders, braided either with pearl or ribbon, perfectly representing the figures of the Graces. I was here convinced of the truth of a reflection I had often made, that if it was the fashion to go naked, the face would be hardly observed.

John Galt, *Letters from the Levant...*, 1813

EPHESUS, 26 April

While the horses are getting ready, I sit down to give you some account of what I have seen to recompense me for the trouble of coming here...

A walk of more than an hour, over broken vaults, and through nettles and briars, effectually cooled the slight desire which I felt to look at objects, of which the era, use, and construction, are equally unknown. The traveller must be far gone in antiquarianism who can admire the wreck of the aqueduct, or the other shapeless heaps that constitute the ruins of Ephesus. To save you the trouble of a search, or the vexation of coming away without accomplishing the objects of your journey, if you are ever so mad as to visit this place, I ought to mention that the remains of the ancient city lie principally along the heights on the West of the modern village; and that those which are now commonly visited as such, are, in fact, of posterior origin, and are perhaps wholly Saracenic.

The situation of Ephesus, as it appears at present, is as well calculated to raise a dispute among topographers as any place that I know. Were I to describe to you only its existing condition – barren rocky hills behind, and a morass of many miles in extent in front, you would not hesitate to say that it must have been extremely ill chosen. But when it is considered that this morass was formed by the inundations of the river having been neglected; that the river, prior to the stoppage by the bar across its mouth, and which is probably of the same date as the morass, was navigable to the city; and that the town stood exactly in that part of the noble and fertile valley of the Castrus, by which it was enabled to unite,

to its maritime advantages, the convenience of an easy communication with the interior, you will perhaps, like me, be disposed to think that it may have been very happily chosen. The marshes round Ephesus are not half so extensive as the levels on the south side of London. Now, were it possible to imagine the modern Babylon desolated; the ruins of the bridges interrupting the course of the Thames; scarcely a vestige of all her thousands of streets and structures remaining; the very site of St Paul's unknown to the miserable inhabitants of a few hovels, half hid by the briars and nettles among the ruins – were it indeed possible to imagine the ruin of London as complete as that of Ephesus – what would then be the state of the low grounds of Vauxhall, Lambeth, and Camberwell, which at present are covered with so many flourishing gardens and terraces? Could they be otherwise than putrid fens, the abodes of reptiles, and the nurseries of pestilence, like those of the plain of Ephesus?

ASIA

BURMA

Somerset Maugham, *A Writer's Notebook*, 1939

Mandalay by moonlight. The white gateways are flooded with silver and the erections above them are shot with silhouetted glimpses of the sky. The effect is ravishing. The moat in Mandalay is one of the minor beauties of the world. It has not the sublimity of Kilauea nor the spectacular picturesque of the Lake of Como, it has not the swooning loveliness of the coastline of a South Pacific island, nor the austere grandeur of parts of the Peloponnesus, but it has a beauty which you can take hold of and enjoy and make your own. It is a beauty which does not carry you off your feet, but which can give you constant delight. Those other beauties need the frame of mind to be enjoyed and appreciated, but this is a beauty suited to all seasons and all moods. It is like Herrick's poems, which you can take up with pleasure when you are out of humour for the *Inferno* or *Paradise Lost*.

CAMBODIA

Richard Halliburton, *The Royal Road to Romance*, 1925

He spoke of it in awesome tones as if it had been a super-human experience. Again and again in India I heard the name linked with superlative adjectives relating to its monstrous size and exquisite detail yet always encompassed in rumor and obscurity. No one there had seen it – everyone said it was a miracle. Angkor – the murmur of its name grew as I moved eastward. Angkor – talks of its name grew as I moved eastward. Angkor – tales of its reputed glories were rumbling in my ears at Bangkok. Angkor – the wind and the jungle and the vast grey cloud of stone roared at me now as I hurried from the bungalow toward the mile-distant mystery: 'Here is the superlative of industry, here the crown of human achievement. Here, here, is Angkor, the first wonder of the world, and the greatest mystery in history.

CHINA
······················

Marco Polo, *The Travels of Marco Polo*, c. 1300

You must know that for three months of the year, to wit December, January, and February, the Great Kaan resides in the capital city of Cathay, which is called CAMBALUC, [and which is at the north-eastern extremity of the country]. In that city stands his great Palace, and now I will tell you what it is like.

It is enclosed all round by a great wall forming a square, each side of which is a mile in length; that is to say, the whole compass thereof is four miles. This you may depend on; it is also very thick, and a good ten paces in height, whitewashed and loop-holed all round. At each angle of the wall there is a very fine and rich palace in which the war-harness of the Emperor is kept, such as bows and quivers, saddles and bridles, and bowstrings, and everything needful for an army. Also midway between every two of these Corner Palaces there is another of the like; so that taking the whole compass of the enclosure you find eight vast Palaces stored with the Great Lord's harness of war. And you must understand that each Palace is assigned to only one kind of article; thus one is stored with bows, a second with saddles, a third with bridles, and so on in succession right round.

The great wall has five gates on its southern face, the middle one being the great gate which is never opened on any occasion except when the Great Kaan himself goes forth or enters. Close on either side of this great gate is a smaller one by which all other people pass; and then towards each angle is another great gate, also open to people in general; so that on that side there are five gates in all.

Inside of this wall there is a second, enclosing a space that is somewhat greater in length than in breadth. This enclosure also has eight palaces corresponding to those of the outer wall, and stored like them with the Lord's harness of war. This wall also

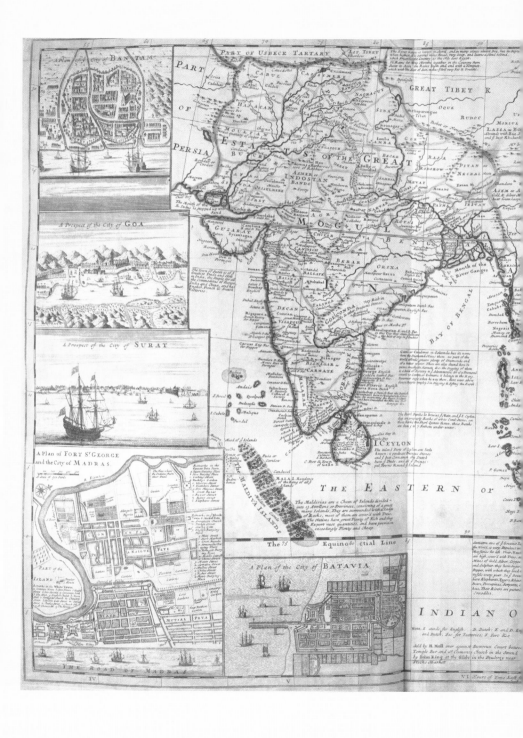

A Plan of the City of BANTAM

A Prospect of the City of GOA

A Prospect of the City of SURAT

A Plan of FORT St GEORGE and the City of MADRAS

THE ROAD OF MADRAS

PART OF USBECK TARTARY

PART OF PERSIA

ESTATES OF THE GREAT

GREAT TIBET

MOGUL

BENGALA

BAY OF BENGAL

CEYLON

THE MALDIVIA ISLANDS

THE EASTERN or

The Equinoctial Line

A Plan of the City of BATAVIA

INDIAN O

hath five gates on the southern face, corresponding to those in the outer wall, and hath one gate on each of the other faces, as the outer wall hath also. In the middle of the second enclosure is the Lord's Great Palace, and I will tell you what it is like.

You must know that it is the greatest Palace that ever was. Towards the north it is in contact with the outer wall, whilst towards the south there is a vacant space which the Barons and the soldiers are constantly traversing. The Palace itself hath no upper story, but is all on the ground floor, only the basement is raised some ten palms above the surrounding soil and this elevation is retained by a wall of marble raised to the level of the pavement, two paces in width and projecting beyond the base of the Palace so as to form a kind of terrace-walk, by which people can pass round the building, and which is exposed to view, whilst on the outer edge of the wall there is a very fine pillared balustrade; and up to this the people are allowed to come. The roof is very lofty, and the walls of the Palace are all covered with gold and silver. They are also adorned with representations of dragons [sculptured and gilt], beasts and birds, knights and idols, and sundry other subjects. And on the ceiling too you see nothing but gold and silver and painting. [On each of the four sides there is a great marble staircase leading to the top of the marble wall, and forming the approach to the Palace.]

The Hall of the Palace is so large that it could easily dine 6000 people; and it is quite a marvel to see how many rooms there are besides. The building is altogether so vast, so rich, and so beautiful, that no man on earth could design anything superior to it. The outside of the roof also is all coloured with vermilion and yellow and green and blue and other hues, which are fixed with a varnish so fine and exquisite that they shine like crystal, and lend a resplendent lustre to the Palace as seen for a great way round. This roof is made too with such strength and solidity that it is fit to last forever.

le mauis temps que il orent et
pour les granu froidures et si
sachies par uerite que quant li
granu caan. sot que mesire ni
colo z mesire mafe pol les mesfa
ges retournoient. il enuoia ses
messages encontre eulx bien
xl iournees. et furent bien ser
ui et honoure par la uoie a la
z tournant de tout ce quel sa
uoient commander. Ci dit le
xiiii. chapitre. Comment mesire
nicole. et mesire mafe. et mart
alerent deuant le grant caan.

deuous en duoie re
quant li doi freres z
mart furent uenu e
cele grant cite silen
alerent au maistre
palais. la ou il trouuerent le grat
seignour a mle grant compaig
nie de barons. Il sagenouillerent
deuant lui. et sumeliberent tat
comme il porent le seignour les
fist dreacer en estant et les recut
mlt honourablement et leur
fist mlt grant ioie z mlt grant
feste z leur demanda moult de
leur estre. et comment il lauoi
ent puis fait. Il respondirent q
il ont mlt bien fait puis que
il ont trouue sain et hantie. A
dont li presenterent les preuile
ges et les chartes que il auoi
ent de par la pastole. Des quels
il ot granu ioie puis li donnerent
la sainte huile du sepulcre et si
mlt liez z les moult cher. Et
quant il uit mart qui estoit
iones bachelers si demanda qui
il estoit. Sire fait son pere mesire
nicolo il est mon filz et uostre
homme. Bien soit il uenu fait
li granu sires. Et pour quoi vo
en feru le lone conte. Sachies
quil y ot fait a la court du seig
nour mlt grant feste de leur ue
nue. et moult estoient bien
serui et honoure: de tous. et
demourerent en la court auec les
autres barons. Ci deuile le xv.
chapitre. Comment le seignor
enuoia mart pour son message.

Rauint que mart le filz
mon seignour nicolo apst
si bien la coustume destatures et
lor langage et lor lettre et lor ar
chier que ce fu merueilles. Et sa
chies vraiement il sot en pou de
temps de plusieurs langages.
et sot de iiii. lettres de lor escrip
tures. il estoit sages z pourueas
en toutes choses. si que pour ce
le seignour li uouloit moult grt
bien. si que quant le seignour
uit quil estoit si sages z de si bian
portement. Si lenuoia en son
message en une terre que bien
y auoit vi. mois de chemin. Luo
nes bacheler fist bien son messa
ge et sagement. et pource quil
auoit plusieurs foiz seu et ueu
que le seignour enuoioit ses
messages par diuerses parties
du monde. Et quant il retour
noient ne li sauoient autre di
re que ce pour quoi il estoient a
le. si les tenoit tous asolz z ani

Arthur Stanley, *The Golden Road*, 1938

Now and then a belated peasant bearing two heavy baskets on his yoke sidles by. The bearers walk more slowly, but after the long day they have lost none of their spirit, and they chatter gaily; they laugh, and one of them breaks into a fragment of tuneless song. But the causeway rises and the lantern throws its light suddenly on a whitewashed wall: you have reached the first miserable houses that straggle along the path outside the city wall, and two or three minutes more bring you to a steep flight of steps. The bearers take them at a run. You pass through the city gates. The narrow streets are multitudinous and in the shops they are busy still. The bearers shout raucously. The crowd divides and you pass through a double hedge of serried curious people. Their faces are impassive and their dark eyes stare mysteriously. The bearers, their day's work done, march with a swinging stride. Suddenly they stop, wheel to the right, into a courtyard, and you have reached the inn. Your chair is set down.

Ian Fleming, *Thrilling Cities*, 1963

As, half-way through the delicious scrambled eggs and bacon, a confiding butterfly, black and cream and dark blue, settled on my wrist, I reflected that heaven could wait. Here, on the green and scarcely inhabited slopes of Shek-O, above Big Wave Bay on the south-east corner of Hong Kong Island, was good enough.

* * *

The streets of Hong Kong are the most enchanting night streets I have trod. Here the advertising agencies are ignorant of the drab fact, known all too well in London and New York, that patterns of black and red and yellow have the most compelling impact on the human eye. Avoiding harsh primary colours, the streets of Hong Kong are evidence that neon lighting need not be hideous, and the crowded Chinese ideograms in pale violet and pink and green with a plentiful use of white are entrancing not only for their colours but also because one does not know what drab messages and exhortations they spell out. The smell of the streets is sea-clean with an occasional exciting dash of sandalwood from a joss-stick factory, frying onions, and the scent of sweet perspiration that underlies Chinese cooking.

GOBI DESERT

Arthur Stanley, *The Golden Road*, 1938

The length of this Desert is so great that 'tis said it would take a year and more to ride from one end of it to the other. And here, where its breadth is least, it takes a month to cross it. 'Tis all composed of hills and valleys of sand, and not a thing to eat is to be found on it. But after riding for a day and a night you find fresh water, enough mayhap for some 50 or 100 persons with their beasts, but not for more. And all across the Desert you will find water in like manner, that is to say, in some 28 places altogether you will find good water, but in no great quantity; and in four places also you find brackish water. Beasts there are none; for there is nought for them to eat. But there is a marvellous thing related of this Desert, which is that when travellers are on the move by night, and one of them chances to lag behind or to fall asleep or the like, when he tries to gain his company again he will hear spirits talking, and will suppose them to be his comrades. Sometimes the spirits will call him by name; and thus shall a traveller oft times be led astray so that he never finds his party. And in this way many have perished. (Sometimes the stray travellers will hear as it were the tramp and hum of a great cavalcade of people away from the real line of road, and taking this to be their own company they will follow the sound; and when day breaks they find that a cheat has been put on them and that they are in an ill plight.) Even in the

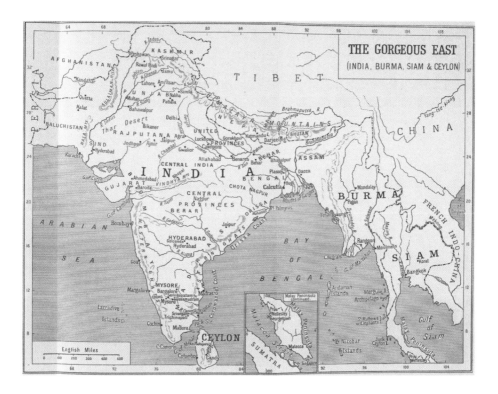

day-time one hears those spirits talking. And sometimes you shall hear the sound of a variety of musical instruments, and still more commonly the sound of drums. [Hence in making this journey 'tis customary for travellers to keep close together. All the animals too have bells at their necks, so that they cannot easily get astray. And at sleeping-time a signal is put up to show the direction of the next march.] So thus it is that the Desert is crossed.

INDIA

Aldous Huxley, *Jesting Pilate: The Diary of a Journey*, 1926

The really odd, unexpected thing about Bombay was its birds. There are more birds in the streets of this million-peopled city than in an English woodland. Huge kites, their wings spread and unmoving, go soaring along the thoroughfares, effortlessly keeping pace with the traffic below. Innumerable grey-headed crows fly hither and thither, sit perched on every roof, every sill and wire. Their cawing is the fundamental bass to every other sound in Bombay. Kites and crows do useful scavenging works, and Bombay which produces much garbage and few dustmen, keeps them well employed and copiously fed. Nobody, in this land where the killing of animals is all but murder, does them or their nests any harm. They increase and multiply, they are astonishingly unafraid. All over India we were to find the same abundance of bird life, the same trustful absence of fear. Coming from Italy, where, for nine months of the year while *lo sport* is in progress, the countryside is almost birdless, where armed men lie ambushed half a day for a hedge-sparrow, and migrant warblers are netted and eaten by the thousand – coming from Italy, I was particularly impressed by the number and variety of Indian birds.

Marianne North, *Recollections of a Happy Life*, 1892

The flowers about Darjeeling seemed endless. I found new ones every day. The Thunbergia coccinea was perhaps the most striking; it twined itself up to the tops of the oaks, and hung down in long tresses of brilliant colour, the oak itself having leaves like the sweet chestnut, and great acorns as big as apricots almost hidden in their cups. There was another lovely creeper peculiar to Darjeeling-the sweet-scented cluster ipomæa, of a pure pink or lilac colour. The wild hydrangea with its tricolour blooms was also much more beautiful than the tame one. I worked so hard and walked so much that, after a dinner or two with Sir Ashley Eden and other grandees, I refused any more invitations.

I could not keep awake in the evening. How I longed to spend a spring in Darjeeling, and to see all the wonderful rhododendrons and magnolias in flower!

* * *

From the hill above Jonboo one saw the plains of Bengal like a sea, and mountains on the other three sides. The clouds rolling in and out of the valleys and up into the sky at sunset, quite took one's breath away with their beauty and colours. They were perfect pillars of fire on some evenings, and one thick cloud with a gold edge, just in front of the setting sun, cast wonderful shadows and rays opposite; but the sky was entirely clear overhead on both nights. The road up passed through grand rhododendrons with gigantic leaves with brown and white linings. The hydrangea,

too, grew into quite a tree here. All the rhododendron trunks were pinkish, some of them quite satin-like and smooth; no moss or ferns could find a hold for their roots in them. Others were covered with creeping things, and the dwarf bamboo came up to the very tops.

Anne Elwood, *Narrative of a journey overland from England, by the continent of Europe, Egypt, and the Red sea, to India*, 1830

Bombay is famed all over the East for its onions which are certainly of a very superior species to our western ones. They are of immense size, and so mild as to be by no means unpleasant in taste and they have not that very disagreeable and almost unbearable smell that the English onions have. The sweet potato is much used, and the common potato, though of late introduction, is gaining ground in India, and it is said, that the prejudice once entertained against it by the natives is quickly passing away.

JAKARTA

François Pelsaert, *Exploring the Mainland*, 1629

Since, on all the islands and cliffs round about our foundered ship "Batavia," there is no freshwater to be found, in order to feed and keep the people who are saved, therefore the commodore has earnestly requested and proposed that an expedition should be made to the main southland to see whether it is God's gracious will that fresh water shall be found, of which so much may be taken to the people that they shall be certain of having enough provision for a considerable time; that then, meanwhile, someone shall be told off to go to Batavia, in order to let the Lord-General and his councillers know of our disaster and to ask him for early assistance. To which we the undersigned have all voluntarily consented, since necessity forces us thereto, and since, if we acted otherwise, we could not answer for our conduct before God and the high authorities. Therefore, we have unanimously agreed and resolved to try the utmost and do our duty and to assist our poor brethren in their great need. In certain knowledge of the truth we have signed this with our own hand, and have all of us sworn to it on the 8th of June, 162. Was signed –

Francois Pelsaert,
Claes Gerritsz,
Jacob Jansz Holoogh,
Claes Jansz Dor,
Adriaen Jacobsz,
Hans Jacobsz Binder,
Jan Evertsz,
Claes Willemsz Graeft,
and Michiel Claesz

* * *

In the afternoon, seeing inland some smoke, they rowed thither, hoping to find an opportunity of landing. They were quite rejoiced, for they imagined that where there were people there would also be fresh water. Having reached the shore, they found the ground to be a steep and rough incline; stony and rocky, against which the breakers beat violently, so that they saw no means of landing. It made them very dejected, for they feared that they would have to depart without landing. At last six men, trusting themselves to their swimming powers jumped overboard, and reached the shore with great difficulty and peril, while the boat remained at anchor outside the breakers in 25 fathoms of water. The swimmers having reached the shore, looked the whole day for fresh water everywhere, till in the evening they became convinced that their search was vain.

They then happened upon four people, who were creeping towards them on their hands and feet. When our men, coming out of a hollow upon a height, suddenly approached them, they leaped to their feet and fled full speed, which was distinctly observed by those in the boat. They were black savages, quite naked, leaving themselves uncovered like animals.

As those on the shore had spent the whole day without finding water, they swam aboard again towards evening being all a good deal hurt and bruised, since the breakers had dashed them roughly against the rocks. Then getting ready and lifting the grappling iron they started in search of a better opportunity, sailing along the coast all night with but little sail, and keeping outside the breakers. On the morning of the 15th, they came to a point where a large reef extended at about a mile from the coast, and, so it seemed, another reef along the shore, so that they tried their best to steer between the two, for the water there appeared to be calm and smooth. But they did not find an entrance until the afternoon, when they saw an opening where there were no breakers. But it was very dangerous, very stony, and often not holding two feet of water. The shore here had a foreland of dunes about a mile broad, before the higher land was reached.

JAPAN

Aldous Huxley, *Jesting Pilate: The Diary of a Journey*, 1926

For a few hours that evening it ceased to rain. We took the opportunity to explore the city on foot. The streets were well lighted, the shops – and almost every one of the hundred thousand shacks in Kyoto is a shop – were mostly open. We walked through the city, seeing the commercial life steadily and seeing it almost whole. It was like walking, ankle-deep in mud, through an enormous Woolworth's bazaar. Such a collection of the cheap and shoddy, of the quasi-genuine and the imitation-solid, of the vulgar and the tawdry, I have never seen. And the strange thing was that, in Kyoto, even the real, the sound, the thoroughly pukka had an air

of flimsiness and falsity. Looking at the most expensive kimonos with a lifetime of wear woven into their thick silk, you would swear that they were things of wood-pulp. The ivories resemble celluloid; the hand embroideries have the appearance of the machine-made article. The genuine antiques – the ones you see in the museums, for there are none elsewhere – look as though they had been fabricated yesterday. This is due partly to the fact that in recent years we have become so familiar with the conventional forms of Japanese art turned out on machines by the million for the penny bazaar market, that we cannot associate them with anything but cheapness and falsity; partly too, I think, to a certain intrinsic feebleness and vulgarity in the forms themselves. That sobriety, that strength, that faultless refinement which are the characteristics of Chinese art, and which give to the cheapest piece of Chinese earthenware, the most ordinary embroidery or carving or lettering, a magistral air of artistic importance and significance, are totally lacking, so it seems to me, in the art of Japan. The designs of Japanese fabrics are garish and pretentious; the sculpture even of the best periods is baroque; the pottery which in China is so irreproachable both in hue and shape is always in Japan just not 'right.' It is as though there were some inherent vice in Japanese art which made the genuine seem false and the expensive shoddy.

Factories, smoke, innumerable Woolworths, mud – were these Japan? We were assured they were not. The 'real' Japan (all countries have a 'real' self, which no stranger can ever hope to see) was something different, was somewhere else.

UZBEKISTAN

Arthur Stanley, *The Golden Road*, 1938

They brought many sheep, cooked and dressed, and a roasted horse, with rice served up in various ways, and much fruit. When they had eaten, they were presented with two horses, a robe, and a hat. The ambassadors were in this garden from Sunday, the 31st of August, to Monday the 8th of September, when the lord sent for them; for it is the custom not to see any ambassador until five or six days are passed, and the more important the ambassador may be, the longer he has to wait.

On Monday, the 8th of September, the ambassadors departed from the garden where they had been lodged, and went to the city of Samarcand. The road went over a plain covered with gardens, and houses, and markets where they sold many things; and at three in the afternoon they came to a large garden and palace, outside the city, where the lord then was. When they arrived, they dismounted, and entered a building outside; where two knights came to them, and said that they were to give up those presents, which they brought for the lord, to certain men who would lay them before him, for such were the orders of the private Meerzas of the lord; so the ambassadors gave the presents to the two knights. They placed the presents in the arms of men who were to carry them respectfully before the lord, and the ambassador from the Sultan did the same with the presents which he brought.

The entrance to this garden was very broad and high, and beautifully adorned with glazed tiles, in blue and gold. At this gate there were many porters, who guarded it, with maces in their hands. When the ambassadors entered, they came to six elephants, with wooden castles on their backs, each of which had two banners,

and there were men on the top of them. The ambassadors went forward, and found the men, who had the presents well arranged on their arms, and they advanced with them in company with the two knights, who held them by the arm pits, and the ambassador whom Timour Beg had sent to the king of Castille was with them; and those who saw him, laughed at him, because he was dressed in the costume and fashion of Castille.

They conducted them to an aged knight, who was seated in an ante-room. He was a son of the sister of Timour Beg, and they bowed reverentially before him. They were then brought before some small boys, grandsons of the lord, who were seated in a chamber, and they also bowed before them.

Here the letter, which they brought from the King to Timour Beg, was demanded, and they presented it to one of these boys, who took it. He was a son of Miran Meerza, the eldest son of the lord. The three boys then got up, and carried the letter to the lord; who desired that the ambassadors should be brought before him.

Timour Beg was seated in a portal, in front of the entrance of a beautiful palace; and he was sitting on the ground. Before him there was a fountain, which threw up the water very high, and in it there were some red apples. The lord was seated cross-legged, on silken embroidered carpets, amongst round pillows. He was dressed in a robe of silk, with a high white hat on his head, on the top of which there was a spinal ruby, with pearls and precious stones round it.

EUROPE

AUSTRIA

Lady Mary Wortley Montagu, *Embassy Letters*, 1716–18

I will keep my promise in giving you an account of my first going to court.

In order to that ceremony, I was squeezed up in a gown, and adorned with a gorget and the other implements thereunto belonging: a dress very inconvenient, but which certainly shews the neck and shape to great advantage. I cannot forbear in this place giving you some description of the fashions here, which are more monstrous and contrary to all common sense and reason, than 'tis possible for you to imagine. They build certain fabrics of gauze on their heads about a yard high, consisting of three or four stories, fortified with numberless yards of heavy ribbon. The foundation of this structure is a thing they call a Bourle, which is exactly of the same shape and kind, but about four times as big, as those rolls our prudent milk-maids make use of to fix their pails upon. This machine they cover with their own hair, which they mix with a great deal of false, it being a particular beauty to have their heads too large to go into a moderate tub. Their hair is prodigiously powdered, to conceal the mixture, and set out with three or four rows of bodkins (wonderfully large, that stick two or three inches from their hair), made of diamonds, pearls, red, green, and yellow stones, that it certainly requires as much art and experience to carry the load upright, as to dance upon May-day with the garland. Their whalebone petticoats outdo ours by several yards circumference, and cover some acres of ground. You may easily suppose how much this extraordinary dress sets off and improves the natural ugliness with which God Almighty has been pleased to endow them all generally. Even the lovely empress herself is obliged to comply, in some degree, with these absurd fashions, which they would not quit for all the world.

BELGIUM

Robert Southey, *Journal of a Tour in the Netherlands in the Autumn of 1815*, 1902

Indeed, this is in very many respects a Frenchified city. The modern part is said to resemble Paris, and the Park is altogether French, with its straight walks and statues, and fountains and shade enough to afford a convenient cover for a profligate people. The town is overrun with splendid carriages; and these, as was notoriously the case in France, are driven without caution or remorse, as if the coachmen wished to terrify or even to run over the foot-passengers.

William Thackeray, *The Paris Sketchbook*, 1840

Whether from my own natural greatness and magnanimity, or from that handsome share of national conceit that every Englishman possesses, my impressions of this city are certainly anything but respectful. It has an absurd kind of Lilliput look with it. There are soldiers, just as in Paris, better dressed, and doing a vast deal of drumming and bustle; and yet, somehow, far from being frightened at them, I feel inclined to laugh in their faces. There are little Ministers, who work at their little bureaux; and to read the journals, how fierce they are! A great thundering Times could hardly talk more big. One reads about the rascally Ministers, the miserable Opposition, the designs of tyrants, the eyes of Europe, &c., just as one would in real journals. The Moniteur of Ghent belabors the Independent of Brussels; the Independent falls foul of the Lynx; and really it is difficult not to suppose sometimes that these worthy people are in earnest.

BRITISH ISLES

ENGLAND

Daniel Defoe, *A Tour Through the Whole Island of Great Britain*, 1724–26

It was, as I say, calm and clear, and the sun shone when we came out of the town of Rochdale; but when we began to mount the hills, which we did within a mile, or little more of the town, we found the wind began to rise, and the higher we went the more wind; by which I soon perceived that it had blown before, and perhaps all night upon the hills, tho' it was calm below; as we ascended higher it began to snow again, that is to say, we ascended into that part where it was snowing, and had, no doubt, been snowing all night, as we could easily see by the thickness of the snow.

CRUCHLEY'S
ENLARGED MAP OF
EUROPE
COMPILED FOR THE USE OF
COLLEGES AND SCHOOLS.
SHOWING THE
PRINCIPAL PHYSICAL FEATURES, &C. &C.

ENGRAVED & PUBLISHED BY G. F. CRUCHLEY, MAP-SELLER, 81 FLEET ST. LONDON.

It is not easy to express the consternation we were in when we came up near the top of the mountain; the wind blew exceeding hard, and blew the snow so directly in our faces, and that so thick, that it was impossible to keep our eyes open to see our way. The ground also was so covered with snow, that we could see no track, or when we were in the way, or when out; except when we were shewed it by a frightful precipice on one hand, and uneven ground on the other; even our horses discovered their uneasiness at it; and a poor spaniel dog that was my fellow traveller, and usually diverted us with giving us a mark for our gun, turn'd tail to it and cry'd.

In the middle of this difficulty, and as we began to call to one another to turn back again, not knowing what dangers might still be before us, came a surprizing clap of thunder, the first that ever I heard in a storm of snow, or, I believe, ever shall; nor did we perceive any lightning to precede the thunder, as must naturally be the case; but we supposed the thick falling of the snow might prevent our sight.

I must confess I was very much surprized at this blow; and one of our company would not be persuaded that it was thunder, but that it was some blast of a coal-pit, things which do sometimes happen in the country, where there are many coal mines. But we were all against him in that, and were fully satisfied that it was thunder, and, as we fancy'd, at last we were confirmed in it, by hearing more of it at a distance from us.

Upon this we made a full stop, and coming altogether, for we were then three in company, with two servants, we began to talk seriously of going back again to Rochdale; but just then one of our men called out to us, and said, he was upon the top of the hill, and could see over into Yorkshire, and that there was a plain way down on the other side.

Daniel Defoe, *From London to Land's End*, 1888

This Yeovil is a market town of good resort, and some clothing is carry'd on, in, and near it, but not much, its main manufacture at this time is making of gloves. It cannot pass my observation here, that when we are come this length from London, the dialect of the English tongue, or the country way of expressing themselves is not easily understood, it is so strangely altered; it is true, that it is so in many parts of England besides, but in none in so gross a degree as in this part; This way of boorish country speech, as in Ireland, it is call'd the brogue upon the tongue; so here 'tis call'd jouring, and 'tis certain, that tho' the tongue be all meer natural English, yet those that are but a little acquainted with them, cannot understand one half of what they say.

Leigh Hunt, 'A "Now";' Descriptive of A Cold Day', *Essays*, 1841

Now sounds in general are dull, and smoke out of chimneys looks warm and rich, and birds are pitied, hopping about for crumbs, and the trees look wiry and cheerless, albeit they are still beautiful to imaginative eyes, especially the evergreens, and the birch with boughs like dishevelled hair. Now mud in roads is stiff, and the kennel ices over, and boys make illegal slides in the pathways, and ashes are strewed before doors; or you crunch the snow as you tread, or kick mud-flakes before you, or are horribly muddy in cities. But if it is a hard frost, all the world is buttoned up and great-coated, except ostentatious elderly gentlemen, and pretended beggars with naked feet; and the delicious sound of 'All hot' is heard from roasted apple and potato stalls, the vendor himself being cold, in spite of his 'hot,' and stamping up and down to warm his feet; and the little boys are astonished to think how he can eat bread and cold meat for his dinner, instead of the smoking apples.

Wilkie Collins, *The Cruise of the Tomtit*, 1855

[of Mangerton-in-the-mud aka Weston-Super-Mare]

The next morning the sky was black, the wind was blowing hard against us, and the waves were showing their white frills angrily in the offing. A double row of spectators had assembled at the jetty, to see us beat out of the bay. If they had come to see us hanged, their grim faces could not have expressed greater commiseration. Our only cheerful farewell came from the doctor and his friend and the two dogs. The remainder of the spectators evidently felt that they were having a last long stare at us, and that it would be indecent and unfeeling, under the circumstances, to look happy. Give me a respectable inhabitant of an English country town, and I will match him, in the matter of stolid and silent staring, against any other man, civilised or savage, over the whole surface of the globe.

[Clovelly, Devon]

About noon we sailed for Clovelly. Our smooth passage across the magnificent Bay of Bideford is the recollection of our happy voyage which I find myself looking back on most lovingly while I now write. No cloud was in the sky. Far away, on the left, sloped inward the winding shore, so clear, so fresh, so divinely tender in its blue and purple hues, that it was the most inexhaustible of luxuries only to look at it. Over the watery horizon, to the right, the autumn sun hung grandly, with the fire-path below, heaving on a sea of lustrous darkest blue. Flocks of wild birds, at rest, floated, chirping on the water all around. The fragrant, steady breeze was just enough to fill our sails. On and on we went, with the bubbling sea-song at our bows to soothe us; on and on, till the blue lustre of the ocean grew darker, till the sun sank redly towards the far waterline, till the sacred evening stillness crept over the sweet air, and hushed it with a foretaste of the coming night. What sight of mystery and enchantment rises before us now? Steep, solemn cliffs, bare in some places – where the dark-red rock has been rent away,

and the winding chasms open grimly to the view–but clothed for the most part with trees, which soften their summits into the sky, and sweep all down them, in glorious masses of wood, to the very water's edge. Climbing from the beach, up the precipitous face of the cliff, a little fishing village coyly shows itself. The small white cottages rise one above another, now perching on a bit of rock, now peeping out of a clump of trees; sometimes two or three together; sometimes one standing alone; here, placed sideways to the sea, there, fronting it, – but rising always one above another, as if instead of being founded on the earth, they were hung from the trees on the top of the cliff. Over all this lovely scene the evening shadows are stealing. The last rays of the sun just tinge the quiet water, and touch the white walls of the cottages. From out at sea comes the sound of a horn, blown from the nearest fishing-vessel, as a signal to the rest to follow her to shore. From the land, the voices of children at play, and the still, faint fall of the small waves on the beach are the only audible sounds. This is Clovelly. If we had travelled a thousand miles to see it, we should have said that our journey had not been taken in vain.

On getting to shore, we found the one street of Clovelly nothing but a succession of irregular steps, from the beginning at the beach, to the end, half-way up the cliffs. It was like climbing to the top of an old castle, instead of walking through a village. When we reached the summit of the cliff, it was getting too dark to see much of the country. We strayed away, however, to look for the church, and found ourselves, at twilight, near some ghastly deserted out-houses, approached by a half-ruinous gate-way, and a damp dark avenue of trees. The church was near, but shut off from us by ivy-grown walls. No living creature appeared; not even a dog barked at us. We were surrounded by silence, solitude, darkness and desolation; and it struck us both forcibly, that the best thing we could do was to give up the church, and get back to humanity with all convenient speed. The descent of the High

Street of Clovelly, at night, turned out to be a matter of more difficulty than we had anticipated. There was no such thing as a lamp in the whole village; and we had to grope our way in the darkness down steps of irregular sizes and heights, paved with slippery pebbles, and ornamented with nothing in the shape of a bannister, even at the most dangerous places. Half-way down, my friend and I had an argument in the dark – standing with our noses against a wall, and with nothing visible on either side – as to which way we should turn next. I guessed to the left, and he guessed to the right; and I, being the most obstinate of the two, we ended in following my route, and at last stumbled our way down to the pier. Looking at the place the next morning, we found that the steps to the right led through a bit of cottage-garden to a snug little precipice, over which inquisitive tourists might pitch quietly, without let or hindrance. Talk of the perils of the deep! What are they in comparison with the perils of the shore?

[The Scilly Isles]

Soon the islands are visible from the deck, and by noon we have run in as near them as we dare without local guidance. They are low-lying, and picturesque in an artistic point of view; but treacherous-looking and full of peril to the wary nautical eye. Horrible jagged rocks, and sinister swirlings and foamings of the sea, seem to forbid the approach to them. The Tomtit is hove to – our ensign is run up half-mast high – and we fire our double-barrelled gun fiercely for a pilot. He arrives in a long, serviceable-looking boat, with a wild, handsome, dark-haired son, and a silent, solemn old man, for his crew. He himself is lean, wrinkled, hungry-looking; his eyes are restless with excitement, and his tongue overwhelms us with a torrent of words, spoken in a strange accent, but singularly free from provincialisms and bad grammar. He informs us that we must have been set to the northward in the night by a current, and goes onto acquaint us with so many other things, with such a fidgetty sparkling of the eyes and such a ceaseless patter of the tongue, that he fairly drives me to the fore part of the vessel out of his way. Smoothly we glide along, parallel with the jagged rocks and the swirling eddies, till we come to a channel between two islands and, sailing through that, make for a sandy isthmus, where we see some houses and a little harbour. This is Hugh Town, the chief place in St. Mary's, which is the largest island of the Scilly group. We jump ashore in high glee, feeling that we have succeeded in carrying out the purpose of our voyage in defiance of the prognostications of all our prudent friends. How sweet is triumph, even in the smallest things!

Bating the one fact of the wind having blown from an unfavourable quarter, unvarying good fortune had, thus far, accompanied our cruise, and our luck did not desert us when we got on shore at St. Mary's. We went, happily for our own comfort, to the hotel kept by the master of the sailing-packet plying between Hugh Town and Penzance. By our landlord and his pleasant, cordial wife and family we were received with such kindness and treated with such care, that we felt really and truly at home before we had been half an hour in the house. And, by way of farther familiarising us with Scilly at first sight, who should the resident medical man turn out to be but a gentleman whom I knew. These were certainly fortunate auspices under which to begin our short sojourn in one of the remotest and wildest places in the Queen's dominions.

The islands seem, at a rough glance, to form a great irregular circle, enclosing a kind of lagoon of sea, communicating by various channels with the main ocean all around. The circumference of the largest of the group is, as we heard, not more than thirteen miles. Five of the islands are inhabited; the rest may be generally described as masses of rock, wonderfully varied in shape and size. Inland, in the larger islands, the earth, where it is not planted or sown, is covered with heather and with the most beautiful ferns. Potatoes used to be the main product of Scilly; but the disease has appeared lately in the island crops, and the potatoes have suffered so severely that, when we filled our sack for the return voyage, we were obliged to allow for two-thirds of our supply proving unfit for use. The views inland are chiefly remarkable as natural pano-ramas of land and sea – the two always presenting themselves intermixed in the loveliest varieties of form and colour. On the coast, the granite rocks, though not notably high, take the most wildly and magnificently picturesque shapes. They are rent into the strangest chasms and piled up in the grandest confusion; and they look down, every here and there, on the loveliest little sandy bays, where the sea, in calm weather, is as tenderly blue and as limpid in its clearness as the Mediterranean itself, The softness and purity of the climate may be imagined, when I state that last winter none of the fresh-water pools were strongly enough frozen to bear being skated on, The balmy sea air blows over each little island as freely as it might blow over the deck of a ship.

The people have the great merit of good manners. We two strangers were so little stared at as we walked about, that it was almost like being on the Continent. The pilot who had taken us into Hugh Town harbour we found to be a fair specimen, as regarded his excessive talkativeness and the purity of his English, of the islanders generally. The longest tellers of very long stories, so far as my experience goes, are to be found in Scilly. Ask the people the commonest question, and their answer generally exhausts the whole subject before you can say another word. Their anxiety, whenever we had occasion to enquire our way, to guard us from the remotest chance of missing it, and the honest pride with which they told us all about local sights and marvels, formed a very pleasant trait in the general character, Strangely enough, in this softest and healthiest of climates consumption is a prevalent disease among the people. If I may venture on an opinion, after a very short observation of their habits, I should say that distrust of fresh air and unwillingness to take exercise were the chief causes of consumptive maladies among the islanders. I longed to break windows in the main street of Hugh Town as I never longed to break them anywhere else. One lovely afternoon I went out for the purpose of seeing how many of the inhabitants of the place had a notion of airing their bedrooms. I found two houses with open windows – all the rest were fast closed from top to bottom, as if a pestilence was abroad instead of the softest, purest, heavenliest sea breeze that ever blew. Then, again, as to walking, the people ask you seriously when you enquire your way on foot, whether you are aware that the destination you want to arrive at is three miles off! As for a pedestrian excursion round the largest island – a circuit of thirteen miles – when we talked of performing that feat in the hearing of a respectable inhabitant, he laughed at the idea as incredulously as if we had proposed a swimming match to the Cornish coast.

Celia Fiennes, *The Illustrated Journeys of Celia Fiennes*, 1698

Kendall is a town built all of stone, one very broad streete in which is the Market Crosse; its a goode tradeing town mostly famed for the Cottons: Kendall Cotton is used for blanckets and the Scotts use them for their Plodds and there is much made here and also Linsiwoolseys, and a great deale of Leather tann'd here, and all sons of Commodityes – twice a weeke is ye market ffurnished wth all sorts of things. The River Can which gives name to the town is pretty Large but full of Rocks and stones that makes shelves and falls in the water, its stor'd wth plenty of good ffish and there are great ffalls of water partly naturall and added to by putting more stones in manner of Wyers, at wrch they Catch Salmon when they Leape with speares. The Roaring of ye water at these places sometymes does foretell wet weather; they do observe when the water roares most in the fall on the Northside it will be ffaire, if on the Southside of the town it will be wet. Some of them are falls as high as a house. The same observation is at Lancaster at the Wires where they Catch Salmon; against Stormes or raines it will be turbulent and Rore as may be heard into the town. There are 3 or 4 good houses in the town, ye rest are like good traders houses very neate and tight. The streetes are all pitch'd which is Extreame Easy to be repair'd, for the whole Country is like one Entire Rock or pitching almost all ye Roads.

SCOTLAND

Samuel Johnson, *A Journey to the Western Islands of Scotland*, 1775

Near the way, by the water side, we espied a cottage. This was the first Highland Hut that I had seen; and as our business was with life and manners, we were willing to visit it. To enter a habitation without leave, seems to be not considered here as rudeness or intrusion. The old laws of hospitality still give this licence to a stranger.

A hut is constructed with loose stones, ranged for the most part with some tendency to circularity. It must be placed where the wind cannot act upon it with violence, because it has no cement; and where the water will run easily away, because it has no floor but the naked ground. The wall, which is commonly about six feet high, declines from the perpendicular a little inward. Such rafters as can be procured are then raised for a roof, and covered with heath, which makes a strong and warm thatch, kept from flying off by ropes of twisted heath, of which the ends, reaching from the center of the thatch to the top of the wall, are held firm by the weight of a large stone. No light is admitted but at the entrance, and through a hole in the thatch, which gives vent to the smoke. This hole is not directly over the fire, lest the rain should extinguish it; and the smoke therefore naturally fills the place before it escapes. Such is the general structure of the houses in which one of the nations of this opulent and powerful island has been hitherto content to live. Huts however are not more uniform than palaces; and this which we were inspecting was very far from one of the meanest, for it was divided into several apartments; and its inhabitants possessed such property as a pastoral poet might exalt into riches.

When we entered, we found an old woman boiling goats-flesh in a kettle. She spoke little English, but we had interpreters at hand; and she was willing enough to display her whole system of economy. She has five children, of which none are yet gone from her. The eldest, a boy of thirteen, and her husband, who is eighty years old, were at work in the wood. Her two next sons were gone to Inverness to buy meal, by which oatmeal is always meant. Meal she considered as expensive food, and told us, that in Spring, when the goats gave milk, the children could live without it. She is mistress of sixty goats, and I saw many kids in an enclosure at the end of her house. She had also some poultry. By the lake we saw a potatoe-garden, and a small spot of ground on which stood four shucks, containing each twelve sheaves of barley. She has all this from the labour of their own hands, and for what is necessary to be bought, her kids and her chickens are sent to market.

With the true pastoral hospitality, she asked us to sit down and drink whisky. She is religious, and though the kirk is four miles off, probably eight English miles, she goes thither every Sunday. We gave her a shilling, and she begged snuff; for snuff is the luxury of a Highland cottage.

Dorothy Wordsworth, *Recollections of a Tour Made in Scotland AD 1803*, 1874

Thursday 25 August

We had not climbed far before we were stopped by a sudden burst of prospect, so singular and beautiful that it was like a flash of images from another world. We stood with our backs to the hill of the island, which we were ascending, and which shut out Ben Lomond entirely, and all the upper part of the lake, and we looked towards the foot of the lake, scattered over with islands without beginning and without end. The sun shone, and the distant hills were visible, some through sunny mists, others in gloom with patches of sunshine; the lake was lost under the low and distant hills, and the islands lost in the lake, which was all in motion with travelling fields of light, or dark shadows under rainy clouds. There are many hills, but no commanding eminence at a

FINE WEATHER

distance to confine the prospect, so that the land seemed endless as the water.

What I had heard of Loch Lomond, or any other place in Great Britain, had given me no idea of anything like what we beheld: it was an outlandish scene – we might have believed ourselves in North America. The islands were of every possible variety of shape and surface – hilly and level, large and small, bare, rocky, pastoral, or covered with wood. Immediately under my eyes lay one large flat island, bare and green, so flat and low that it scarcely appeared to rise above the water, with straggling peat-stacks and a single hut upon one of its out-shooting promontories – for it was of a very irregular shape, though perfectly flat. Another, its next neighbour, and still nearer to us, was covered over with heath and coppice-wood, the surface undulating, with flat or sloping banks towards the water, and hollow places, cradle-like valleys, behind. These two islands, with Inch-ta-vanach, where we were standing, were intermingled with the water, I might say interbedded and interveined with it, in a manner that was exquisitely pleasing. There were bays innumerable, straits or passages like calm rivers, landlocked lakes, and, to the main water, stormy promontories.

The solitary hut on the flat green island seemed unsheltered and desolate, and yet not wholly so, for it was but a broad river's breadth from the covert of the wood of the other island. Near to these is a miniature, an islet covered with trees, on which stands a small ruin that looks like the remains of a religious house; it is overgrown with ivy, and were it not that the arch of a window or gateway may be distinctly seen, it would be difficult to believe that it was not a tuft of trees growing in the shape of a ruin, rather than a ruin overshadowed by trees. When we had walked a little further we saw below us, on the nearest large island, where some of the wood had been cut down, a hut, which we conjectured to be a bark hut. It appeared to be on the shore of a little forest lake, enclosed by Inch-ta-vanach, where we were, and the woody island on which the hut stands.

Beyond we had the same intricate view as before, and could discover Dumbarton rock with its double head. There being a mist over it, it had a ghost-like appearance – as I observed to William and Coleridge, something like the Tor of Glastonbury from the Dorsetshire hills. Right before us, on the flat island mentioned before, were several small single trees or shrubs, growing at different distances from each other, close to the shore, but some optical delusion had detached them from the land on which they stood, and they had the appearance of so many little vessels sailing along the coast of it.

NORTHERN IRELAND

William Thackeray, *The Irish Sketch Book 1843*, 1843

If the road from Larne to Glenarm is beautiful, the coast route from the latter place to Cushendall is still more so; and, except peerless Westport, I have seen nothing in Ireland so picturesque as this noble line of coast scenery. The new road, luckily, is not yet completed, and the lover of natural beauties had better hasten to the spot in time, ere, by flattening and improving the road, and leading it along the sea-shore, half the magnificent prospects are shut out, now visible from along the mountainous old road; which, according to the good old fashion, gallantly takes all the hills in its course, disdaining to turn them. At three miles' distance, near the village of Cairlough, Glenarm looks more beautiful than when you are close upon it; and, as the car travels on to the stupendous Garron Head, the traveller, looking back, has view of the whole line of coast southward as far as Isle Magee, with its bays and white villages, and tall precipitous cliffs, green, white, and gray. Eyes left, you may look with wonder at the mountains rising above, or presently at the pretty park and grounds of Drumnasole. Here, near the woods of Nappan, which are dressed in ten thousand colours – ash-leaves turned yellow, nut-trees red, birch-leaves brown, lime-leaves speckled over with black Spots (marks of a disease which they will never get over) – stands a school-house that looks like a French chateau, having probably been a villa in former days, and discharges as we pass a cluster of fair-haired children, that begin running madly down the hill, their fair hair streaming behind them. Down the hill goes the car, madly too, and you wonder and bless your stars that the horse does not fall, or crush the children that are running before, or you that are sitting behind. Every now and then, at a trip of the horse, a disguised lady's-maid, with a canary-bird in her lap and a vast anxiety about her best bonnet in the band-box, begins to scream: at which the car-boy grins, and rattles down the hill only the quicker. The road, which almost always skirts the hill-side, has been torn sheer through the rock here and there: an immense work of leveling, shovelling, picking, blasting, filling, is going on along the whole line. As I was looking up a vast cliff, decorated with patches of green here and there at its summit, and at its base, where the sea had beaten until now, with long, thin, waving grass, that I told a grocer, my neighbour, was like mermaid's hair (though he did not in the least coincide in the simile) – as I was looking up the hill, admiring two goats that were browsing on a little patch of green, and two sheep perched yet higher (I had never seen such agility in mutton) as I say once more, I was looking at these phenomena, the grocer nudges me and says, 'Look on to this side – that's Scotland yon.' If ever this book reaches a second edition, a sonnet shall be inserted in this place, describing the author's feelings on HIS FIRST VIEW OF SCOTLAND. Meanwhile, the Scotch Mountains remain undisturbed, looking blue and solemn, far away in the placid sea.

CROATIA

Rebecca West, *Black Lamb and Grey Falcon: A Journey Through Yugoslavia*, 1941

'This is Zagreb!' cried the Germans, and took all their luggage down from the racks, then they broke into excessive cries of exasperation and distress because it was not Zagreb, it was Zagreb-Sava, a suburb three or four miles out of the main town, I leaned out of the window. Rain was falling heavily, and the mud shone between the railway tracks. An elderly man, his thin body clad in a tight-fitting, flimsy overcoat, trotted along beside the train, crying softly, 'Anna! Anna! Anna!' He held an open umbrella not over himself but at arm's length. He had not brought it for himself, but for the beloved woman he was calling. He did not lose

hope when he found her nowhere in all the long tram, but turned and trotted all the way back, calling still with anxious sweetness, 'Anna! Anna! Anna!' When the train steamed out he was trotting along it a third time, holding his umbrella still further away from him. A ray of light from an electric standard shone on his white hair, on the dome of his umbrella, which was streaked with several rents, and on the strong spears of the driving ram. I was among people I could understand.

CYPRUS

John Sibthorp, *Voyage in the Grecian Seas*, 1820

We now entered the vale of Soulea, the most beautiful we had yet seen in the island; well watered and richly cultivated. Green meadows contrasted with the corn now ripe, hamlets shaded with mulberry-trees, and healthy peasantry busily employed with their harvest, and the care of their silk-worms, enlivened the scenery. Having travelled two hours in this delightful vale, I stopped at a Greek village. My guide conducted me to the house of the Papas; a bed was prepared for me in the vacant part of a chamber where silk-worms were kept.

FRANCE

Charles Dickens, *Pictures from Italy*, 1846

There is little more than one variety in the appearance of the country, for the first two days. From a dreary plain, to an interminable avenue, and from an interminable avenue, to a dreary plain again. Plenty of vines there are, in the open fields, but of a short low kind, and not trained in festoons, but about straight sticks. Beggars innumerable there are, everywhere; but an extraordinarily scanty population, and fewer children than I ever encountered. I don't believe we saw a hundred children between Paris and Chalons. Queer old towns, draw-bridged and walled: with odd little towers at the angles, like grotesque faces, as if the wall had put a mask on, and were staring, down into the moat; other Strange little towers, in gardens and fields, and down lanes, and in farm-yards: all alone, and always round, with a peaked roof, and never used for any purpose at all; ruinous buildings of all sorts: sometimes an hôtel de Ville, sometimes a guard-house, sometimes a dwelling-house, sometimes a chateau with a rank garden, prolific in dandelion, and watched over by extinguisher-topped turrets, and blink-eyed little casements; are the standard objects, repeated over and over again. Sometimes we pass a village inn, with a crumbling wall belonging to it, and a perfect town of out-houses: and painted over the gateway, Stabling for Sixty Horses; as indeed there might be stabling for sixty score, were there any horses to be stabled there, or anybody resting there, or anything stirring about the place but a dangling bush, indicative of the wine inside: which flutters idly in the wind, in lazy keeping with everything else, and certainly is never in a green old age, though always so old age to be dropping to pieces.

And all day long, strange little narrow waggons, in strings of six or eight, bringing cheese from Switzerland, and frequently in charge, the whole line, of one man or even boy – and he very often asleep in the foremost cart – come jingling past: the horses drowsily ringing the bells upon their harness, and looking as if they thought (no doubt they do) their great blue woolly furniture, of immense weight and thickness with a pair of grotesque horns growing out of the collar, very much too warm for the Midsummer weather.

Henry James, *A Little Tour in France*, 1884

There are two shabby old inns at Arles, which compete closely for your custom. I mean by this that if you elect to go to the Hotel du Forum, the Hotel du Nord, which is placed exactly beside it (at a right angle) watches your arrival with ill-concealed disapproval; and if you take the chances of its neighbor, the Hotel du Forum seems to glare at you invidiously from all its windows and doors. I forget which of these establishments I selected; whichever it was, I wished very much that, it had been the other. The two stand together on the Place des Hommes, a little public square of Arles, which somehow quite misses its effect. As a city, indeed, Arles quite misses its effect in every way; and if it is a charming place, as I think it is, I can hardly tell the reason why. The straight-nosed Arlesiennes account for it in some degree; and the remainder may

be charged to the ruins of the arena and the theatre. Beyond this, I remember with affection the ill-proportioned little Place des Hommes; not at all monumental, and given over to puddles and to shabby cafes.

I recall with tenderness the tortuous and featureless streets, which looked like the streets of a village, and were paved with villanous little sharp stones, making all exercise penitential. Consecrated by association is even a tiresome walk that I took the evening I arrived, with the purpose of obtaining a view of the Rhone. I had been to Arles before, years ago, and it seemed to me that I remembered finding on the banks of the stream some sort of picture. I think that on the evening of which I speak there was a watery moon, which it seemed to me would light up the past as well as the present. But I found no picture, and I scarcely found the Rhone at all. I lost my way, and there was not a creature in the streets to whom I could appeal. Nothing could be more provincial than the situation of Arles at ten o'clock at night. At last I arrived at a kind of embankment, where I could see the great mud-colored stream slipping along in the soundless darkness. It had come on to rain, I know not what had happened to the moon, and the whole place was anything but gay. It was not what I had looked for; what I had looked for was in the irrecoverable past.

I groped my way back to the inn over the infernal *cailloux*, feeling like a discomfited Dogberry. I remember now that this hotel was the one (whichever that may be) which has the fragment of a Gallo-Roman portico inserted into one of its angles. I had chosen it for the sake of this exceptional ornament. It was damp and dark, and the floors felt gritty to the feet; it was an establishment at which the dreadful *gras-double* might have appeared at the table d'hote, as it had done at Narbonne. Nevertheless, I was glad to get back to it; and nevertheless, too, – and this is the moral of my simple anecdote, – my pointless little walk (I don't speak of the pavement) suffuses itself, as I look back upon it, with a romantic tone. And in relation to the inn, I suppose I had better mention that I am well aware of the inconsistency of a person who dislikes the modern caravansary, and yet grumbles when he finds a hotel of the superannuated sort.

One ought to choose, it would seem, and make the best of either alternative. The two old taverns at Arles are quite unimproved; such as they must have been in the infancy of the modern world, when Stendhal passed that way, and the lumbering diligence deposited him in the Place des Hommes, such in every detail they are to-day. *Vieilles auberges de France*, one ought to enjoy their gritty floors and greasy window-panes. Let it be put on record, therefore, that I have been, I won't say less comfortable, but at least less happy, at better inns.

George Orwell, *Down and Out in Paris and London*, 1933

It was a very narrow street – a ravine of tall leprous houses, lurching towards one another in queer attitudes, as though they had all been frozen in the act of collapse. All the houses were hotels and packed to the tiles with lodgers, mostly Poles, Arabs and Italians. At the foot of the hotels were tiny bistros, where you could be drunk for the equivalent of a shilling. On Saturday nights about a third of the male population of the quarter was drunk. There was fighting over women, and the Arab navvies who lived in the cheapest hotels used to conduct mysterious feuds, and fight them out with chairs and occasionally revolvers. At night the policemen would only come through the street two together. It was a fairly rackety place. And yet amid the noise and diff lived the usual respectable French shopkeepers, bakers and laundresses and the like, keeping/ themselves to themselves and quietly piling up small fortunes. It was quite a representative Paris slum.

Benjamin Franklin, letter to Mary Stevenson, Paris, 14 September 1767

I had not been here Six Days before my Taylor and Peruquier had transform'd me into a Frenchman. Only think what a Figure I make in a little Bag Wig and naked Ears! They told me I was become 20 Years younger, and look'd very galante; so being in Paris where the Mode is to be sacredly follow'd, I was once very near making Love to my Friend's Wife.

Elizabeth Barrett Browning, letter to Miss E.F. Haworth, 23 July 1858

Paris is so full of life – murmurs so of the fountain of intellectual youth for ever and ever – that rolling up the Rue de Rivoli (much more the Boulevards) suggests a quicker beat of the fancy's heart, and I like it – I like it. The architectural beauty is wonderful. Give me Venice on water, Paris on land – each in its way is a dream city.

George Sand, letter to Gustave Flaubert, 21 September 1866

We are a little fed up with dolmens and menhirs and we have fallen on fetes and have seen costumes which they said had been

58. Curious Menhir on the plain of Ménec, near Carnac, (p. 205.)

suppressed but which the old people still wear. Well! These men of the past are ugly with their home-spun trousers, their long hair, their jackets with pockets under the arms, their sottish air, half drunkard, half saint. And the Celtic relics, uncontestably curious for the archaeologist, have naught for the artist, they are badly set, badly composed, Carnac and Erdeven have no physiognomy. In short, Brittany shall not have my bones! I prefer a thousand times your rich Normandy, or, in the days when one has dramas in his HEAD, a real country of horror and despair. There is nothing in a country where priests rule and where Catholic vandalism has passed, razing monuments of the ancient world and sowing the plagues of the future.

e. e. cummings, *Eimi*, 1933

[On a train from Paris to Moscow]

Twilight—a wet rolling land of gentle & infinite darkness … a little silhouette with a lantern, himself dissolved in universal … a bird, reading the air… (what spirits go & come? curiously into Whom are we all unpossibly melting?)

[Paris train bound for Moscow via Poland]

Go somewhere and do something my excited fellowsufferer complains in several languages simultaneously. Something?—ah, the ticket, from here to Moscow: l go and I do: but what a ticketless ticket! So, in dream moving, preceded by trifles, through very gate of inexorably has a magic wand been waved; miraculously did reality disintegrate: where am I? in a world of Was—everything shoddy; everywhere dirt and cracked fingernails—guarded by 1 helplessly handsome implausibly immaculate soldier. Look! A rickety train, centuries BC. Tiny rednosed genial antique wasman, swallowed by outfit of patches, nods almost merrily as I climb cautiously aboard. My suitcase knapsack typewriter gradually are heaved (each by each) into a lofty alcove; leaving this massive barrenness of compartment much more than merely empty (a kissing sickle and hammer sink in heaver's palm, almost child trickles away).

Tobias Smollett, *Travels Through France and Italy*, 1766

We set out from Lyons early on Monday morning, and as a robbery had been a few days before committed in that neighbourhood, I ordered my servant to load my musquetoon with a charge of eight balls. By the bye, this piece did not fail to attract the curiosity and admiration of the people in every place through which we passed.

The carriage no sooner halted, than a crowd immediately surrounded the man to view the blunderbuss, which they dignified with the title of petit canon. At Nuys in Burgundy, he fired it in the air, and the whole mob dispersed, and scampered off like a flock of sheep. In our journey hither, we generally set out in a morning at eight o'clock, and travelled till noon, when the mules were put up and rested a couple of hours. During this halt, Joseph went to dinner, and we went to breakfast, after which we ordered provision for our refreshment in the coach, which we took about three or four in the afternoon, halting for that purpose, by the side of some transparent brook, which afforded excellent water to mix with our wine. In this country I was almost poisoned with garlic, which they mix in their ragouts, and all their sauces; nay, the smell of it perfumes the very chambers, as well as every person you approach. I was also very sick of beccaficas, grieves, or thrushes, and other little birds, which are served up twice a day at all ordinaries on the road. They make their appearance in vine-leaves, and are always half raw, in which condition the French choose to eat them, rather than run the risk of losing the juice by over-roasting.

Épinal

And there are many other things in which Épinal is wonderful, but in nothing is it more wonderful than in its great church.

I suppose that the high Dukes of Burgundy and Lorraine and the rich men from Flanders and the House of Luxemburg and the rest, going to Rome, the centre of the world, had often to pass up this valley of the Moselle, which (as I have said) is a road leading to Rome, and would halt at épinal and would at times give money for its church; with this result, that the church belongs to every imaginable period and is built anyhow, in twenty styles, but stands as a whole a most enduring record of past forms and of what has pleased the changing mind when it has attempted to worship in stone.

Thus the transept is simply an old square barn of rough stone, older, I suppose, than Charlemagne and without any ornament.

In its lower courses I thought I even saw the Roman brick. It had once two towers, northern and southern; the southern is ruined and has a wooden roof, the northern remains and is just a pinnacle or minaret too narrow for bells.

Then the apse is pure and beautiful Gothic of the fourteenth century, with very tall and fluted windows like single prayers. The ambulatory is perfectly modern, Gothic also, and in the manner that Viollet le Duc in France and Pugin in England have introduced to bring us back to our origins and to remind us of the place whence all we Europeans came. Again, this apse and ambulatory are not perpendicular to the transept, but set askew, a thing known in small churches and said to be a symbol, but surely very rare in large ones. The western door is purely Romanesque, and has Byzantine ornaments and a great deep round door. To match it there is a northern door still deeper, with rows and rows of inner arches full of saints, angels, devils, and flowers; and this again is not straight, but so built that the arches go aslant, as you sometimes see railway bridges when they cross roads at an angle. Finally, there is a central tower which is neither Gothic nor Romanesque but pure Italian, a loggia, with splendid round airy windows taking up all its walls, and with a flat roof and eaves.

This some one straight from the south must have put on as a memory of his wanderings.

The barn-transept is crumbling old grey stone, the Romanesque porches are red, like Strasburg, the Gothic apse is old white as our cathedrals are, the modern ambulatory is of pure white stone just quarried, and thus colours as well as shapes are mingled up and different in this astonishing building.

I drew it from that point of view in the market-place to the north-east which shows most of these contrasts at once, and you must excuse the extreme shakiness of the sketch, for it was taken as best I could on an apple-cart with my book resting on the apples – there was no other desk. Nor did the apple-seller mind my doing it, but on the contrary gave me advice and praise saying such things as –

'Excellent; you have caught the angle of the apse … Come now, darken the edge of that pillar … I fear you have made the tower a little confused,' and so forth.

I offered to buy a few apples off him, but he gave me three instead, and these, as they incommoded me, I gave later to a little child.

Indeed the people of Épinal, not taking me for a traveller but simply for a wandering poor man, were very genial to me, and the best good they did me was curing my lameness. For, seeing an apothecary's shop as I was leaving the town, I went in and said to the apothecary –

'My knee has swelled and is very painful, and I have to walk far; perhaps you can tell me how to cure it, or give me something that will.'

'There is nothing easier,' he said; 'I have here a specific for the very thing you complain of.'

With this he pulled out a round bottle, on the label of which was printed in great letters, 'BALM'.

'You have but to rub your knee strongly and long with this ointment of mine,' he said, 'and you will be cured.' Nor did he mention any special form of words to be repeated as one did it. Everything happened just as he had said. When I was some little way above the town I sat down on a low wall and rubbed my knee strongly and long with this balm, and the pain instantly disappeared. Then, with a heart renewed by this prodigy, I took the road again and began walking very rapidly and high, swinging on to Rome.

GERMANY

Ann Radcliffe, *A Journey Made in the Summer of 1794...*, 1795

Cologne

Now we began to experience the inconveniences of its neighbourhood to the seat of war, some of which had appeared at Bonn from the arrival of families, who could not be lodged in the former place. We were no sooner within the gates, than the throng of people and carriages in a city, which only a few weeks before was almost as silent as gloomy, convinced us we should not find a very easy welcome. The sentinels, when they made the usual enquiry as to our inn, assured us, that there had been no lodgings at the Hotel de Prague for several days, and one of them followed us, to see what others we should find. Through many obstructions by military and other carriages, we, however, reached this inn, and were soon convinced that there could be no room, the landlord shewing us the chaises in which some of his guests slept, and his billiard table already loaden with beds for others.

There was so much confusion meanwhile in the adjoining square, that, upon a slight assurance, we could have believed the French to be within a few miles of the city, and have taken refuge on the opposite bank of the Rhine. At length, our host told us, that what he believed to be the worst room in the place was still vacant, but might not be so half an hour longer. We followed his man to it, in a distant part of the city, and saw enough in our way of parties taking refreshment in carriages, and gentlemen carrying their own baggage, to make us contented with a viler cabin than any person can have an idea of, who has not been out of England. The next morning we heard from the mistress of it how fortunately we had been situated, two or three families having passed the night in the open market-place, and great numbers in their carriages.

Charlie Chaplin, *My Wonderful Visit*, 1922

[travelling by train from Paris to Berlin]

Our compartment in the train is very stuffy and smelly, and the train service is atrocious, food and sanitary conditions being intolerable after American train service.

* * *

I notice that the Germans seem to be scrupulously honest, or maybe this was all the more noticeable to me because of genial and unsuspicious treatment by a taxi driver. We left the cab many times and were gone as long as half an hour at a time, and out of sight, yet he always waited and never suggested that he be paid beforehand.

Alice Meynell, 'The Watershed: Lines written between Munich and Verona', 1901

Black mountains pricked with pointed pine
  A melancholy sky.
Out-distanced was the German vine,
  The sterile fields lay high.
From swarthy Alps I travelled forth
Aloft; it was the north, the north;
  Bound for the Noon was I.

I seemed to breast the streams that day;
  I met, opposed, withstood
The northward rivers on their way,
  My heart against the flood–
My heart that pressed to rise and reach,
And felt the love of altering speech,
  of frontiers, in its blood.

But O the unfolding South! the burst
  of summer! O to see
of all the southward brooks the first!
  The travelling heart went free
With endless streams; that strife was stopped;
And down a thousand vales I dropped,
  I flowed to Italy.

Mary Shelley, *History of a Six Weeks' Tour*, 1817

We were carried down by a dangerously rapid current, and saw on either side of us hills covered with vines and trees, craggy cliffs crowned by desolate towers, and wooded islands, where pictur-esque ruins peeped from behind the foliage, and cast the shadows of their forms on the troubled waters, which distorted without deforming them. We heard the songs of the vintagers, and if surrounded by disgusting Germans, the sight was not so replete with enjoyment as I now fancy it to have been; yet memory, taking all the dark shades from the picture, presents this part of the Rhine to my remembrance as the loveliest paradise on earth.

GREECE

Herodotus, *The History*, 440 BCE

[Describing the Royal Road, which crossed the Persian Empire]

Now the true account of the road in question is the following: Royal stations exist along its whole length, and excellent caravanserais; and throughout, it traverses an inhabited tract, and is free from danger. In Lydia and Phrygia there are twenty stations within a distance of 94 ½ parasangs. On leaving Phrygia the Halys has to be crossed; and here are gates through which you must needs pass ere you can traverse the stream. A strong force guards this post. When you have made the passage, and are come into Cappadocia, 28 stations and 104 parasangs bring you to the borders of Cilicia, where the road passes through two sets of gates, at each of which there is a guard posted. Leaving these behind, you go on through Cilicia, where you find three stations in a distance of 15 ½ parasangs. The boundary between Cilicia and Armenia is the river Euphrates, which it is necessary to cross in boats. In Armenia the resting-places are 15 in number, and the distance is 56 ½ parasangs. There is one place where a guard is posted. Four large streams intersect this district, all of which have to be crossed by means of boats. The first of these is the Tigris; the second and the third have both of them the same name, though they are not only different rivers, but do not even run from the same place. For the one which I have called the first of the two has its source in Armenia, while the other flows afterwards out of the country of the Matienians. The fourth of the streams is called the Gyndes, and this is the river which Cyrus dispersed by digging for it three hundred and sixty channels. Leaving Armenia and entering the Matienian country, you have four stations; these passed you find yourself in Cissia, where eleven stations and 42 ½ parasangs bring you to another navigable stream, the Choaspes, on the banks of which the city of Susa is built. Thus the entire number of the stations is raised to one hundred and eleven; and so many are in fact the resting-places that one finds between Sardis and Susa. If then the royal road be measured aright, and the parasang equals, as it does, thirty furlongs, the whole distance from Sardis to the palace of Memnon (as it is called), amounting thus to 450 parasangs, would be 13,500 furlongs. Travelling then at the rate of 150 furlongs a day, one will take exactly ninety days to perform the journey.

Christopher Marlowe, *The Jew of Malta*, 1590

Content, but we will leave this paltry land,
And sail from hence to Greece, to lovely Greece:
I'll be thy Jason, thou my golden fleece;
Where painted carpets o'er the meads are hurled,
And Bacchus' vineyards overspread the world,
Where woods and forests go in goodly green,
I'll be Adonis, thou shalt be Love's Queen.

Sir Walter Raleigh, letter to Lady Raleigh, 9 April 1898

Corfu is after all a dead place, and Athens a consolation for lost happiness. There is nothing alive in the Parthenon. You feel this acutely when you wander round the ancient Greek theatre with a small and vulgar crowd of English, Americans and Germans and their pettifogging sentiments. Once, no doubt, Ajax took his farewell of the sun in that theatre while a people that understood listened. I have no use for these decaying twigs of antiquity except when I can build my nest of them…The ancient Greeks were a fine people, but that does not enable the modern mountain-goat

to jump off its own shadow. So it spends its life, and imagines that it succeeds, never having tasted reality. Ancient ruins are really only a sauce to heighten the enjoyment of those who relish flat, low, dull modern life.

IRELAND

William Thackeray, *The Irish Sketch Book*, 1843

The papers being read, it became my duty to discover the town; and a handsomer town with fewer people in it, it is impossible to see on a summer's day.

In the whole wide square of Stephen's Green, I think there were not more than two nursery-maids, to keep company with the statue of George 1., who rides horse-back in the middle of the garden, the horse having his foot up to trot, as if he wanted to go out of town too. Small troops of dirty children (too poor and dirty to have lodgings at Kingstown) were squatting here and there upon the sunshiny steps, the only clients at the thresholds of the professional gentlemen, whose names figure on brass plates on the doors. A stand of lazy carmen, – a policeman or two with clinking boot-heels, a couple of moaning beggars leaning against the rails, and calling upon the Lord, and a fellow with a toy and book stall, where the lives of St. Patrick, Robert Emmett, and Lord Edward Fitzgerald, may be bought for double their value, were all the population of the Green.

At the door of the Kildare-street Club I saw eight gentlemen looking at two boys playing at leap-frog: at the door of the University six lazy porters, in jockey caps, were sunning themselves on a bench – a sort of blue-bottle race; and the Bank on the opposite side did not look as if sixpence-worth of change had been negotiated there during the day. There was a lad pretending to sell umbrellas under the colonnade, almost the only instance of trade going on; and I began to think of Juan Fernandez, or Cambridge in the long vacation. In the courts of the College, scarce the ghost of a gyp or the shadow of a bedmaker. In spite of the solitude, the square of the College is a fine sight – a large ground, surrounded by buildings of various ages and styles, but comfortable, handsome, and in good repair; a modern row of rooms; a row that has been Elizabethan once; a hall and senate-house, facing each other, of the style of George I.; and a noble library, with a range of many windows, and a fine manly, simple facade of cut stone. The library was shut. The librarian, I suppose, is at the sea-side; and the only part of the establishment which I could see, was the museum, to which one of the jockey-capped porters conducted me, up a wide, dismal staircase, (adorned with an old pair of jack-boots, a dusty canoe or two, a few helmets, and a South Sea Islander's armour), which passes through a hall hung round with cobwebs, (with which the blue-bottles are too wise to meddle), into an old mouldy room, filled with dingy glass-cases, under which the articles of curiosity or science, were partially visible.

* * *

On leaving Ballynahinch, (with sincere regret, as any lonely tourist may imagine, who is called upon to quit the hospitable friendliness of such a place and society,) my way lay back to Clifden again, and thence through the Joyce country, by the Killery mountains, to Westport, in Mayo. The road, amounting in all to four-and-forty Irish miles, is performed in cars, in different periods of time, according to your horse and your luck. Sometimes, both being bad, the traveller is two days on the road; sometimes a dozen hours will suffice for the journey, which was the case with me, though I confess to having found the twelve hours long enough.

After leaving Clifden, the friendly look of the country seemed to vanish; and, though picturesque enough, was a thought too wild and dismal for eyes accustomed to admire a hop-garden in

Kent, or a view of rich folly meadows in Surrey, with a clump of trees and a comfortable village spire. Inglis,' the Guide-book says, 'compares the scenes to the Norwegian Fiords.' Well, the Norwegian Fiords must, in this case, be very dismal sights! and I own that the wildness of Hampstead Heath (with the imposing walls of Jack Straw's Castle rising stern in the midst of the green wilderness), are more to my taste than the general views of yesterday. We skirted by lake after lake, lying lonely in the midst of lonely boglands, or bathing the sides of mountains robed in sombre rifle green.

Two or three men, and as many huts, you see in the course of each mile, perhaps; as toiling up the bleak hills, or jingling more rapidly down them, you pass through this sad region. In the midst of the wilderness, a chapel stands here and there, solitary on the hill-side; or a ruinous, useless school-house, its pale walls contrasting with the general surrounding hue of sombre purple and green. But though the country looks more dismal than Connemara, it is clearly more fertile: we passed miles of ground that evidently wanted but little cultivation to make them profitable; and along the mountain sides, in many places, and over a great extent of Mr. Blake's country especially, the hills were covered with thick, natural plantation, that may yield a little brushwood now, but might in fifty years' time bring thousands of pounds of revenue to the descendants of the Blakes. My spectacle of a country going to waste is enough to make the cheerfullest landscape look dismal; it gives this wild district a woeful look indeed. The names of the lakes by which we came I noted down in a pocket-book as we passed along; but the names were Irish, the car was rattling, and the only name readable in the catalogue is Letterfrack.

The little hamlet of Leenane is at twenty miles' distance from Clifden; and to arrive at it, you skirt the mountain along one side of a vast pass, through which the ocean runs from Killery Bay, separating the mountains of Mayo from the mountains of Galway. Nothing can be more grand and gloomy than this pass; and as

for the character of the Scenery, it must, as the Guide-book says, be seen to be understood.' Meanwhile, let the reader imagine huge, dark mountains, in their accustomed livery of purple and green, a dull gray sky above them, an estuary silver bright below: in the water lies a fisherman's boat or two; a pair of sea-gulls, undulating with the little waves of the water; a pair of curlews wheeling overhead, and piping on the wing, and on the hill-side a jingling car, with a cockney in it, oppressed by, and yet admiring, all these things. Many sketcher and tourist, as I found, has visited this picturesque spot; for the hostess of the inn had stories of English and American painters and of illustrious book-writers too.

ITALY

J. W. von Goethe, *Letters from Italy*, 1817

Perugia, Oct. 25, 1786

It was a beautiful evening, and I now turned to descend the mountain. As I was proceeding along the Roman road, calm and composed, suddenly I heard behind me some rough voices in dispute. I fancied that it was only the Sbirri, whom I had previously noticed in the town. I therefore went on without care, but still with my ears listening to what they might be saying behind me. I soon became aware that I was the object of their remarks. Four men of this body (two of whom were armed with guns) passed me in the rudest way possible, muttering to each other, and, turning back after a few steps, suddenly surrounded me. They demanded my name, and what I was doing there. I said that I was a stranger, and had travelled on foot to Assisi while my *vetturino* had gone on to Foligno. It appeared to them very improbable that any one should pay for a carriage, and yet travel on foot. They asked me if I had been visiting the Gran Convento. I answered 'No,' but assured them that I knew the building of old; but, being an architect, my chief object this time was simply to obtain a sight of the Maria della Minerva, which, they must be aware, was an architectural model. This they could not contradict, but seemed to take it very ill that I had not paid a visit to the saint, and avowed their suspicion that probably my business was to smuggle contraband goods. I pointed out to them how ridiculous it was that a man who walked openly through the streets, alone, and without packs, and with empty pockets, should be taken for a contrabandist.

However, upon this I offered to return to the town with them, and to go before the *podestà*, and, by showing my papers, prove to him that I was an honest traveller. Upon this they muttered together for a while, and then expressed their opinion that it was unnecessary; and as I behaved throughout with coolness and gravity, they at

last left me, and turned toward the town. I looked after them. As
these rude churls moved on in the foreground, behind them the
beautiful Temple of Minerva once more caught my eye to soothe
and console me with its sight. I turned then to the left, to look at
the heavy Cathedral of St. Francisco, and was about to continue
my way, when one of the unarmed Sbirri separating himself from
the rest, came up to me in a quiet and friendly manner. Saluting
me, he said, 'Signior stranger, you ought at least to give me something to drink your health; for I assure you, that, from the very
first, I took you to be an honourable man, and loudly maintained
this opinion in opposition to my comrades. They, however, are
hot-headed and over-hasty fellows, and have no knowledge of
the world. You yourself must have observed that I was the first to
allow the force of, and to assent to, your remarks.' I praised him
on this score, and urged him to protect all honourable strangers
who might henceforward come to Assisi for the sake either of
religion or of art, and especially all architects who might wish to
do honour to the town by measuring and sketching the temple of
Minerva, since a correct drawing or engraving of it had never yet
been taken. If he were to accompany them, they would, I assured
them, give him substantial proofs of their gratitude; and with these
words I put into his hand some silver, which, as exceeding his
expectation, delighted him above measure. He begged me to pay a
second visit to the town; remarking that I ought not on any account
to miss the festival of the saint, on which I might with the greatest
safety, delight and amuse myself. Indeed, if, being a good-looking
fellow, I should wish to be introduced to the fair sex, he assured
me that the prettiest and most respectable ladies would willingly
receive me, or any stranger, upon his recommendation. He took
his leave, promising to remember me at vespers before the tomb
of the saint, and to offer up a prayer for my safety throughout my
travels. Upon this we parted, and most delighted was I to be again
alone with nature and myself. The road to Foligno was one of the

most beautiful and agreeable walks that I ever took. For four full hours I walked along the side of a mountain, having on my left a richly cultivated valley.

John Evelyn, *The Diary of John Evelyn*, c. 1645

From hence, I returned to Padua, when that town was so infested with soldiers, that many houses were broken open in the night, some murders committed, and the nuns next our lodging disturbed, so as we were forced to be on our guard with pistols and other fire-arms to defend our doors; and indeed the students themselves take a barbarous liberty in the evenings when they go to their strumpets, to stop all that pass by the house where any of their companions in folly are with them. This custom they cali chi vali, so as the streets are very dangerous, when the evenings grow dark; nor is it easy to reform this intolerable usage, where there are so many strangers of several nations.

Using to drink my wine cooled with snow and ice, as the manner here is, I was so afflicted with an angina and sore-throat, that it had almost cost me my life. After all the remedies Cavalier Veslingius, chief professor here, could apply, old Salvatieo (that famous physician) being called. made me be cupped, and scarified in the back in four places; which began to give me breath, and consequently life; for I was in the utmost danger; but, God being merciful to me, I was after a fortnight abroad again; when, changing my lodging, I went over against Pozzo Pinto, where I bought for winter provision 3000 weight of excellent grapes, and pressed my own wine, which proved incomparable liquor.

Hilaire Belloc, *The Path to Rome*, 1902

Lucca

For all my early start, the intolerable heat had again taken the ascendant before I had fairly entered the plain. Then, it being yet but morning, I entered from the north the town of Lucca, which is the neatest, the regularest, the exactest, the most fly-in-amber little town in the world, with its uncrowded streets, its absurd fortifications, and its contented silent houses – all like a family at ease and at rest under its high sun. It is as sharp and trim as its own map, and that map is as clear as a geometrical problem. Everything in Lucca is good.

* * *

Siena

I awoke in the station of Siena, where the railway ends and goes no farther.

It was still only morning; but the glare was beyond bearing as I passed through the enormous gate of the town, a gate pierced in high and stupendous walls that are here guarded by lions. In the narrow main street there was full shade, and it was made cooler by the contrast of the blaze on the higher storeys of the northern side. The wonders of Siena kept sleep a moment from my mind. I saw their great square where a tower of vast height marks the guildhall. I heard Mass in a chapel of their cathedral: a chapel all frescoed, and built, as it were, out of doors, and right below the altar-end or choir. I noted how the city stood like a queen of hills dominating all Tuscany: above the Elsa northward, southward above the province round Mount Amiato. And this great mountain I saw also hazily far off on the horizon. I suffered the vulgarities of the main street all in English and American, like a show. I took my money and changed it; then, having so passed not a full hour, and oppressed by weariness, I said to myself: 'After all, my business is not with cities, and already I have seen far off the great hill whence one can see far off the hills that overhang Rome.'

With this in my mind I wandered out for a quiet place, and found it in a desolate green to the north of the city, near a huge, old red-brick church like a barn. A deep shadow beneath it invited me in spite of the scant and dusty grass, and in this country no one disturbs the wanderer. There, lying down, I slept without dreams till evening.

Charles Dickens, *Pictures from Italy*, 1846

Hard by here is a large Palazzo, formerly belonging to some member of the Brignole family, but just now hired by a school of Jesuits for their summer quarters. I walked into its dismantled precincts the other evening about sunset, and couldn't help pacing up and down for a little time, drowsily taking in the aspect of the place: which is repeated hereabouts in all directions.

I loitered to and fro, under a colonnade, forming two sides of a weedy, grass-grown court-yard, whereof the house formed a third side, and a low terrace-walk, overlooking the garden and the neighbouring hills, the fourth. I don't believe there was an uncracked stone in the whole pavement. In the centre was a

melancholy statue, so piebald in its decay, that it looked exactly as if it had been covered with sticking-plaster, and afterwards powdered. The stables, coach-houses, offices, were all empty, all ruinous, all utterly deserted.

Doors had lost their hinges, and were holding on by their latches; windows were broken, painted plaster had peeled off, and was lying about in clods; fowls and cats had so taken possession of the out-buildings, that I couldn't help thinking of the fairy tales, and eyeing them with suspicion, as transformed retainers, waiting to be changed back again. One old Tom in particular: a scraggy brute, with a hungry green eye (a poor relation, in reality, I am inclined to think): came prowling round and round me, as if he half believed, for the moment, that I might be the hero come to marry the lady, and set all to-rights; but discovering his mistake, he suddenly gave a grim snarl, and walked away with such a tremendous tail, that he couldn't get into the little hole where he lived, but was obliged to wait outside, until his indignation and his tail had gone down together.

In a soft of summer-house, or whatever it may be, in this colonnade, some Englishmen had been living, like grubs in a nut; but the Jesuits had given them notice to go, and they had gone, and that was shut up too. The house: a wandering, echoing, thundering banack of a place, with the lower windows barred up, as usual, was wide open at the door: and I have no doubt I might have gone in, and gone to bed, and gone dead, and nobody a bit the wiser. Only one suite of rooms on an upper floor was tenanted; and from one of these, the voice of a young-lady vocalist, practising bravura lustily, came flaunting out upon the silent evening.

* * *

In the luxurious wonder of so rare a dream, I took but little heed of time, and had but little understanding of its flight. But there were days and nights in it; and when the sun was high, and when the rays of lamps were crooked in the running water, I was still afloat, I thought: plashing the slippery walls and houses with the cleavings of the tide, as my black boat, borne upon it, skimmed along the streets.

Sometimes, alighting at the doors of churches and vast palaces, I wandered on, from room to room, from aisle to aisle, through labyrinths of rich altars, ancient monuments; decayed apartments where the furniture, half awful, half grotesque, was mouldering away. Pictures were there, replete with such enduring beauty and expression: with such passion, truth, and power: that they seemed so many young and fresh realities among a host of spectres. I thought these often intermingled with the old days of the city: with its beauties, tyrants, captains, patriots, merchants, courtiers, priests: nay, with its very stones, and bricks, and public places; all of which lived again, about me, on the walls. Then, coming down some marble staircase where the water lapped and oozed against the lower steps, I passed into my boat again, and went on in my dream.

Floating down narrow lanes, where carpenters, at work with plane and chisel in their shops, tossed the light shaving straight upon the water, where it lay like weed, or ebbed away before me in a tangled heap. Past open doors, decayed and rotten from long steeping in the wet, through which some scanty patch of vine shone green and bright, making unusual shadows on the pavement with its trembling leaves. Past quays and terraces, where women, gracefully veiled, were passing and repassing, and where idlers were reclining in the sunshine, on flagstones and on flights of steps. Past bridges, where there were idlers too: loitering and looking over. Below stone balconies, erected at a giddy height, before the loftiest windows of the loftiest houses. Past plots of garden, theatres, shrines, prodigious piles of architecture – Gothic – Saracenic – fanciful with all the fancies of all times and countries. Past buildings that were high, and low, and black, and white,

and straight, and crooked; mean and grand, crazy and strong. Twining among a tangled lot of boats and barges, and shooting out at last into a Grand Canal! There, in the errant fancy of my dream, I saw old Shylock passing to and fro upon a bridge, all built upon with shops and humming with the tongues of men; a form I seemed to know for Desdemona's, leaned down through a latticed blind to pluck a flower. And, in the dream, I thought that Shakespeare's spirit was abroad upon the water somewhere: stealing through the city.

At night, when two votive lamps burnt before an image of the

Virgin, in a gallery outside the great cathedral, near the roof, I fancied that the great piazza of the Winged Lion was a blaze of cheerful light, and that its whole arcade was thronged with people; while crowds were diverting themselves in splendid coffee-houses opening from it – which were never shut, I thought, but open all night long. When the bronze giants struck the hour of midnight on the bell, I thought the life and animation of the city were all centred here; and as I rowed away, abreast the silent quays, I only saw them dotted, here and there, with sleeping boatmen wrapped up in their cloaks, and lying at full length upon the stones.

But, close about the quays and churches, palaces and prisons: sucking at their walls, and welling up into the secret places of the town: crept the water always. Noiseless and watchful: coiled round and round it, in its many folds, like an old serpent: waiting for the time, I thought, when people should look down into its depths for any stone of the old city that had claimed to be its mistress.

Thus it floated me away, until I awoke in the old market-place at Verona. I have, many and many a time, thought since, of this strange Dream upon the water: half-wondering if it lie there yet, and if its name be VENICE.

Vernon Lee, *Limbo and Other Essays*, 1897

That smell was mysteriously connected with it; the smell of wine-vats mingled, I fancy (though I could not say why), with the sweet faint smell of decaying plaster and wood-work. One night, as we were driving through Bologna to wile away the hours between two trains, in the blue moon-mist and deep shadows of the black porticoed city, that same smell came to my nostrils as in a dream, and with it a whiff of bygone years, the years when first I had had this impression of Italian Magic. Oddly enough, Rome, where I spent much of my childhood and which was the object of my childish and tragic adoration, was always something apart, never Italy for my feelings. The Apennines of Lucca and Pistoia, with their sudden revelation of Italian fields and lanes, of flowers on wall and along roadside, of bells ringing in the summer sky, of peasants working in the fields and with the loom and distaff, meant Italy.

But how much more Italy – and hence longed for how much! – was Lucca, the town in the plain, with cathedral and palaces. Nay, any of the mountain hamlets where there was nothing modern, and where against the scarred brick masonry and blackened stonework the cypresses rose black and tapering, the trelisses crawled bright green up hill! One never feels, once out of childhood, such joy as on the rare occasions when I was taken to such places. A certain farmhouse, with cypresses at the terrace corner and a great oleander over the wall, was also Italy before it became my home for several years. Most of all, however, Italy was represented by certain towns: Bologna, Padua and Vicenza, and Siena, which I saw mainly in the summer.

It is curious how one's associations change: nowadays Italy means mainly certain familiar effects of light and cloud, certain exquisitenesses of sunset amber against ultramarine hills, of winter mists among misty olives, of folds and folds of pale blue

mountains; it is a country which belongs to no time, which will always exist, superior to picturesqueness and romance. But that is but a vague, half-indifferent habit of enjoyment. And every now and then, when the Midsummer Magic is rife, there comes to me that very different, old, childish meaning of the word; as on that day among the roses of those Benedictine cloisters, the cool shadow of the fig-trees in the yards, with the whiff of that queer smell, heavy with romance, of wine-saturated oak and crumbling plaster; and I know with a little stab of joy that this is Italy.

Percy Bysshe Shelley, letter to Leigh Hunt, 1818

There are two Italies; one composed of the green earth & transparent sea and the mighty ruins of ancient times, and aerial mountains, & the warm & radiant atmosphere which is interfused through all things. The other consists of the Italians of the present day, their works & ways. The one is the most sublime & lovely contemplation that can be conceived by the imagination of man; the other the most degraded, disgusting & odious. – What do you think? Young women of rank actually eat – you will never guess what – garlic. Our poor friend Lord Byron is quite corrupted by living among these people; & in fact is going on in a way not very worthy of him.

Hester Lynch Piozzi, *Observations and Reflections Made in the Course of a Journey through France, Italy, and Germany*, 1789

This city seems really under admirable regulations; here are fewer beggars than even at Florence, where however one for fifty in the states of Genoa or Venice do not meet your eyes. And either the word liberty has bewitched me, or I see an air of plenty without insolence, and business without noise, that greatly delight me. Here is much cheerfulness too, and gay good-humour; but this is the season of devotion at Lucca, and in these countries the ideas of devotion and diversion are so blended, that all religious worship seems connected with, and to me now regularly implies, a festive show.

Well, as the Italians say, 'Il mondo e bello perche e variabile.' We English dress our clergymen in black, and go ourselves to the theatre in colours. Here matters are reversed, the church at noon looked like a flower-garden, so gaily adorned were the priests, confrairies, etc., while the opera-house at night had more the air of a funeral, as everybody was dressed in black: a circumstance I had forgotten the meaning of, till reminded that such was once the emulation of finery among the persons of fashion in this city, that it was found convenient to restrain the spirit of expense, by obliging them to wear constant mourning: a very rational and well-devised rule in a town so small, where everybody is known to everybody; and where, when this silly excitement to envy is wisely removed, I know not what should hinder the inhabitants from living like those one reads of in the Golden Age; which, above all others, this climate most resembles, where pleasure contributes to soothe life, commerce to quicken it, and faith extends its prospects to eternity. Such is, or such at least appears to me this lovely territory of Lucca: where cheap living, free government, and genteel society may be enjoyed with a tranquillity unknown to larger states; where there are delicious and salutary baths a few miles out of town, for the nobility to make villeggiatura at; and where, if those nobility were at all disposed to cultivate and communicate learning, every opportunity for study is afforded.

D.H. Lawrence, *Twilight in Italy*, 1916

The school-mistress had told me I should find snowdrops behind San Tommaso. If she had not asserted such confident knowledge I should have doubted her translation of perce-neige. She meant Christmas roses all the while.

However, I went looking for snowdrops. The walls broke down

suddenly, and I was out in a grassy olive orchard, following a track beside pieces of fallen overgrown masonry. So I came to skirt the brink of a steep little gorge, at the bottom of which a stream was rushing down its steep slant to the lake. Here I stood to look for my snowdrops. The grassy, rocky bank went down steep from my feet. I heard water tittle-tattling away in deep shadow below. There were pale flecks in the dimness, but these, I knew, were primroses. So I scrambled down.

Looking up, out of the heavy shadow that lay in the cleft, I could see, right in the sky, grey rocks shining transcendent in the pure empyrean. 'Are they so far up?' I thought. I did not dare to say, 'Am I so far down?' But I was uneasy. Nevertheless it was a lovely place, in the cold shadow, complete; when one forgot the shining rocks far above, it was a complete, shadowless world of shadow. Primroses were everywhere in nests of pale bloom upon the dark, steep face of the cleft, and tongues of fern hanging out, and here and there under the rods and twigs of bushes were tufts of wrecked Christmas roses, nearly over, but still, in the coldest corners, the lovely buds like handfuls of snow.

There had been such crowded sumptuous tufts of Christmas roses everywhere in the stream-gullies, during the shadow of winter that these few remaining flowers were hardly noticeable.

I gathered instead the primroses that smelled of earth and of the weather. There were no snowdrops. I had found the day before a bank of crocuses, pale, fragile, lilac-coloured flowers with dark veins, pricking up keenly like myriad little lilac-coloured flames among the grass, under the olive trees. And I wanted very much to find the snowdrops hanging in the gloom. But there were not any.

I gathered a handful of primroses, then I climbed suddenly, quickly out of the deep watercourse, anxious to get back to the sunshine before the evening fell. Up above I saw the olive trees in their sunny golden grass, and sunlit grey rocks immensely high up. I was afraid lest the evening would fall whilst I was groping

about like an otter in the damp and the darkness, that the day of sunshine would be over.

Soon I was up in the sunshine again, on the turf under the olive trees, reassured. It was the upper world of glowing light, and I was safe again. All the olives were gathered, and the mills were going night and day, making a great, acrid scent of olive oil in preparation, by the lake. The little stream rattled down. A mule driver 'Hued!' to his mules on the Strada Vecchia. High up, on the Strada Nuova, the beautiful, new, military high-road, which winds with beautiful curves up the mountain-side, crossing the same stream several times in clear-leaping bridges, travelling cut out of sheer slope high above the lake, winding beautifully and gracefully forward to the Austrian frontier, where it ends: high up on the lovely swinging road, in the strong evening sunshine, I saw a bullock wagon moving like a vision, though the clanking of the wagon and the crack of the bullock whip resounded close in my ears.

Everything was clear and sun-coloured up there, clear-grey rocks partaking of the sky, tawny grass and scrub, browny-green spires of cypresses, and then the mist of grey-green olives fuming down to the lake-side. There was no shadow, only clear sun-substance built up to the sky, a bullock wagon moving slowly in the high sunlight, along the uppermost terrace of the military road. I sat in the warm stillness of the transcendent afternoon.

Elizabeth Barrett Browning, letter to Miss Mitford, 1854

To leave Rome will fill me with barbarian complacency. I don't pretend to have a ray of sentiment about Rome. It's a palimpsest Rome, a watering-place written over the antique, and I haven't taken to it as a poet should I suppose.

SICILY

D.H. Lawrence, *Sea and Sardinia*, 1921

Here in Sicily it is so pleasant: the sunny Ionian sea, the changing jewel of Calabria, like a fire-opal moved in the light; Italy and the panorama of Christmas clouds, night with the dog-star laying a long, luminous gleam across the sea, as if baying at us, Orion marching above; how the dog-star Sirius looks at one, looks at one! he is the hound of heaven, green, glamorous and fierce! – and then oh regal evening star, hung westward flaring over the jagged dark precipices of tall Sicily: then Etna, that wicked witch, resting her thick white snow under heaven, and slowly, slowly rolling her orange-coloured smoke. They called her the Pillar of Heaven, the Greeks. It seems wrong at first, for she trails up in a long, magical, flexible line from the sea's edge to her blunt cone, and does not seem tall. She seems rather low, under heaven. But as one knows her better, oh awe and wizardry! Remote under heaven, aloof, so near, yet never with us. The painters try to paint her, and the photographers to photograph her, in vain. Because why? Because the near ridges, with their olives and white houses, these are with us. Because the river-bed, and Naxos under the lemon groves, Greek Naxos deep under dark-leaved, many-fruited lemon groves, Etna's skirts and skirt-bottoms, these still are our world, our own world. Even the high villages among the oaks, on Etna. But Etna herself, Etna of the snow and secret changing winds, she is beyond a crystal wall. When I look at her, low, white, witch-like under heaven, slowly rolling her orange smoke and giving sometimes a breath of rose-red flame, then I must look away from earth, into the ether, into the low empyrean. And there, in that remote region, Etna is alone. If you would see her, you must slowly take off your eyes from the world and go a naked seer to the strange chamber of the empyrean. Pedestal of heaven! The Greeks had a sense of the magic truth of things. Thank goodness one still knows enough about them to find one's kinship at last. There are so many photographs, there are so infinitely many water-colour drawings and oil paintings which purport to render Etna. But pedestal of heaven! You must cross the invisible border. Between the foreground, which is our own, and Etna, pivot of winds in lower heaven, there is a dividing line. You must change your state of mind. A metempsychosis. It is no use thinking you can see and behold Etna and the foreground both at once. Never. One or the other. Foreground and a transcribed Etna. Or Etna, pedestal of heaven.

Why, then, must one go? Why not stay? Ah, what a mistress, this Etna! with her strange winds prowling round her like Circe's panthers, some black, some white. With her strange, remote communications and her terrible dynamic exhalations. She makes men mad. Such terrible vibrations of wicked and beautiful electricity she throws about her, like a deadly net! Nay, sometimes, verily, one can feel a new current of her demon magnetism seize one's living tissue and change the peaceful life of one's active cells. She makes a storm in the living plasm and a new adjustment. And sometimes it is like a madness.

This timeless Grecian Etna, in her lower-heaven loveliness, so lovely, so lovely, what a torturer! Not many men can really stand her, without losing their souls. She is like Circe. Unless a man

is very strong, she takes his soul away from him and leaves him not a beast, but an elemental creature, intelligent and soulless. Intelligent, almost inspired, and soulless, like the Etna Sicilians. Intelligent daimons, and humanly, according to us, the most stupid people on earth. Ach, horror! How many men, how many races, has Etna put to flight? It was she who broke the quick of the Greek soul. And after the Greeks, she gave the Romans, the Normans, the Arabs, the Spaniards, the French, the Italians, even the English, she gave them all their inspired hour and broke their souls.

SARDINIA

D.H. Lawrence, *Sea and Sardinia*, 1921

After a really good meal we went out to see the town. It was after three o'clock and everywhere was shut up like an English Sunday. Cold, stony Cagliari: in summer you must be sizzling hot, Cagliari, like a kiln. The men stood about in groups, but without the intimate Italian watchfulness that never leaves a passer-by alone.

Strange, stony Cagliari. We climbed up a street like a corkscrew stairway. And we saw announcements of a children's fancy-dress ball. Cagliari is very steep. Half-way up there is a strange place called the bastions, a large, level space like a drill-ground with trees, curiously suspended over the town, and sending off a long shoot like a wide viaduct, across above the corkscrew street that comes climbing up. Above this bastion place the town still rises steeply to the Cathedral and the fort. What is so curious is that this terrace or bastion is so large, like some big recreation ground, that it is almost dreary, and one cannot understand its being suspended in midair. Down below is the little circle of the harbour. To the left a low, malarial-looking sea plain, with tufts of palm trees and Arab-looking houses. From this runs out the long spit of land towards that black-and-white watch-fort, the white road trailing forth.

On the right, most curiously, a long strange spit of sand runs in a causeway far across the shallows of the bay, with the open sea on one hand, and vast, end-of-the-world lagoons on the other. There are peaky, dark mountains beyond this – just as across the vast bay are gloomy hills. It is a strange, strange landscape: as if here the world left off. The bay is vast in itself; and all these curious things happening at its head: this curious, craggy-studded town, like a great stud of house-covered rock jutting up out of the bay flats: around it on one side the weary, Arab-looking palm-desolated malarial plain, and on the other side great salt lagoons, dead beyond the sand-bar: these backed again by serried, clustered mountains, suddenly, while away beyond the plain, hills rise to sea again. Land and sea both seem to give out, exhausted, at the bay head: the world's end. And into this world's end starts at Cagliari, and on either side, sudden, serpent-crested hills.

But it still reminds me of Malta: lost between Europe and Africa and belonging to nowhere. Belonging to nowhere, never having belonged to anywhere. To Spain and the Arabs and the Phoenicians most. But as if it had never really had a fate. No fate. Left outside of time and history.

The spirit of the place is a strange thing. Our mechanical age tries to override it. But it does not succeed. In the end the strange, sinister spirit of the place, so diverse and adverse in differing places, will smash our mechanical oneness into smithereens, and all that we think the real thing will go off with a pop, and we shall be left staring.

THE NETHERLANDS

John Evelyn, *The Diary of John Evelyn*, c. 1645

We arrived late at Rotterdam, where was their annual mart or fair, so furnished with pictures, (especially landscapes and drolleries, as they call those clownish representations,) that I was amazed. Some of these I bought, and sent into England. The reason of this store of pictures, and their cheapness, proceeds from their want of land to employ their stock, so that it is an ordinary thing to find a common farmer lay out two or three thousand pounds in this commodity. Their houses are full of them, and they vend them at their fairs to very great gains. Here I first saw an elephant... and a pelican.

Oliver Goldsmith, *A Briton in Holland*, 1754

Their pleasures here are very dull tho very various. You may smoak you may doze: you may go to the Italian comedy as good an amusement as either of the former. This entertainment always brings in Harlequin who is generally a Magician and in consequence of his Diabolicall art performs a thousand tricks on the rest of the persons of the drama who are all fools. I have seen the pit in a roar of laughter at his humour when with his sword he touches the glass another was drinking from, 'twas not his face they laughd at for that was maskd, they must have seen something vastly queer in the wooden sword that neither I nor you Sr were you there cou'd see. In winter, when their cannals are frozen every house is forsaken and all People are on the ice. Sleds drawn by horses and skating are at that time the reigning amusements. They have boats here that slide on the ice and are driven by the winds. When they spread all their sails they go more than a mile and an half a minite. Their motion is so rapid that the Eye can scarce accompany them. Their ordinary manner of Travelling is very cheap and very convenient. They sail in coverd boats drawn by horses and in these you are sure to meet people of all nations. Here the Dutch slumber the French chatter and the English play cards, any man who likes company may have them to his Taste. For my part I generally detachd myself from all society and was wholy Taken up in observing the face of the country, nothing can

Equall its beauty. Wherever I turn my Eye fine houses elegant gardens statues grottoes vistas present themselvs but enter their Towns and you are charmd beyond description. No no[th]ing can be more clean [or beau]tiful.

PORTUGAL

Lord Byron, letter to Rev F. Hodgson, 1809

I am very happy here because I loves oranges, and talks bad Latin to the Monks, who understand it as it is like their own. And I goes into society (with my pocket pistols) and I swims in the Tagus all across at once, and I rides on an ass or a mule and swears Portuguese, and I have got a diarrhoea, and bites from the mosquitoes. But what of that? Comfort must not be expected by folks that go a-pleasuring.

William Beckford, *Italy, Spain and Portugal*, 1835

We have a homely saying, that what is poison to one man is meat to another, and true enough; for these days and nights of

glowing temperature, which oppress me beyond endurance, are the delight and boast of the inhabitants of this capital. The heat seems not only to have new venomed the stings of the fleas and the musquitoes, but to have drawn out, the whole night long, all the human ephemera of Lisbon. They frisk, and dance, and tinkle their guitars from sunset to sunrise. The dogs, too, keep yelping and howling without intermission; and what with the bellowing of litanies by parochial processions, the whizzing of fireworks, which devotees are, perpetually letting off in honour of some member or other of the celestial hierarchy, and the squabbles of bullying rake-hells, who scour the streets in search of adventures, there is no getting a wink of sleep, even if the heat would allow it.

As to those quiet nocturnal parties, where ingenuous youths rest their heads, not on the lap of earth, but on that of their mistresses, who are soothingly employed in delivering the jetty locks of their lovers from too abundant a population, I have nothing to say against them, nor am I much disturbed by the dashing sound of a few downfalls from the windows; but these dog-howlings exceed every annoyance of the kind I ever endured, and give no slight

foretaste of the infernal regions.

Nothing but amusement and racket being thought of here at this season (when to celebrate St. Peter's festival with all the noise and extravagance in your power, is not more a profane inclination than a pious duty), that simpleton, the Conde de Villa Nova, opened his garden last night to the nob and mobility of Lisbon.

RUSSIA

e. e. cummings, *Eimi*, 1933

Opposite the Lenin institute(opposite the aggressively unreal boxlike structure pompously,with a toy's pomposity,flying a red flag)there's a pseudo-square;in this squareless square people scurry,nonmen and men;through all these people circling vertiginously a rickety automobile street-sprinkler–with the sprinkle going full tilt–ploughs. Men-and-nonmen stumbling rush thither and hither;some get drenched,some merely spattered;all are threatened,several escape. Not 1 scurrier,however, registers anything approximating indignation

(and–from safety of sidewalk–Can't pointed,chortling)it can't be turned off. That's Russia!

the actuality of which metaphor gives me pause. I actually feel(at that moment)how perfectly the far famed revolution of revolutions resembles a running amok streetsprinkler,a normally benevolent mechanism which attains–thanks(possibly)to some defect in its construction or(possibly)to the ignorance or (probably)playfulness of its operator–distinct if spurious loss of unimportance;certain transient capacity for clumsily mischievous behavior…very naturally whereupon occur trivial and harmless catastrophes

The store was shut.

SPAIN

Leonard Woolf, 'The Real Spain', *Essays on Literature, History, Politics etc.*, 1927

The superficial vivacity and excitability of the Southerner conceals the fact that the Spaniard lives slowly and meditatively. In a Spanish posada you sit after dinner round a wood fire with the inn-keeper and his family, the 'boots' and the carrier, and the conversation is only an interval between long silences in which everyone meditatively stares into the glowing embers. The Spaniard, in fact, belongs to a Europe which had not invented the steam engine, or rather, perhaps, he belongs, not to Europe at all, but to the East, where men talk quickly but live slowly, cultivating their gardens and moving at the same pace as their camels or their bullock carts.

Washington Irving, *The Alhambra*, 1832

For nearly three months had I enjoyed undisturbed my dream of sovereignty in the Alhambra: a longer term of quiet than had been the lot of many of my predecessors. During this lapse of time the progress of the season had wrought the usual change. On my arrival I had found every thing in the freshness of May; the foliage of the trees was still tender and transparent; the pomegranate had not yet shed its brilliant crimson blossoms; the orchards of the Xenil and the Darro were in full bloom; the rocks were hung with wild flowers, and Granada seemed completely surrounded by a wilderness of roses; among which innumerable nightingales sang, not merely in the night, but all day long.

Now the advance of summer had withered the rose and silenced the nightingale, and the distant country began to look parched and sunburnt; though a perennial verdure reigned immediately round the city and in the deep narrow valleys at the foot of the snow-capped mountains.

The Alhambra possesses retreats graduated to the heat of the

weather, among which the most peculiar is the almost subterranean
apartment of the baths. This still retains its ancient Oriental
character, though stamped with the touching traces of decline.
At the entrance, opening into a small court formerly adorned
with flowers, is a hall, moderate in size, but light and graceful
in architecture. It is overlooked by a small gallery supported by
marble pillars and Morisco arches. An alabaster fountain in the
centre of the pavement still throws up a jet of water to cool the
place. On each side are deep alcoves with raised platforms, where
the bathers, after their ablutions, reclined on cushions, soothed
to voluptuous repose by the fragrance of the perfumed air and
the notes of soft music from the gallery. Beyond this hall are the
interior chambers, still more retired; the sanctum sanctorum of
female privacy; for here the beauties of the Harem indulged in
the luxury of the baths. A soft mysterious light reigns through the
place, admitted through small apertures (lumbreras) in the vaulted
ceiling. The traces of ancient elegance are still to be seen; and the
alabaster baths in which the sultanas once reclined. The prevailing
obscurity and silence have made these vaults a favorite resort of
bats, who nestle during the day in the dark nooks and corners, and on

being disturbed, flit mysteriously about the twilight chambers, heightening, in an indescribable degree, their air of desertion and decay.

In this cool and elegant, though dilapidated retreat, which had the freshness and seclusion of a grotto, I passed the sultry hours of the day as summer advanced, emerging towards sunset, and bathing, or rather swimming, at night in the great reservoir of the main court. In this way I was enabled in a measure to counteract the relaxing and enervating influence of the climate.

My dream of absolute sovereignty, however, came at length to an end. I was roused one morning by the report of fire-arms, which reverberated among the towers as if the castle had been taken by surprise. On sallying forth, I found an old cavalier with a number of domestics, in possession of the Hall of Ambassadors. He was an ancient count who had come up from his palace in Granada to pass a short time in the Alhambra for the benefit of purer air, and who, being a veteran and inveterate sportsman, was endeavoring to get an appetite for his breakfast by shooting at swallows from the balconies. It was a harmless amusement; for though, by the alertness of his attendants in loading his pieces, he was enabled to keep up a brisk fire, I could not accuse him of the death of a single swallow. Nay, the birds themselves seemed to enjoy the sport, and to deride his want of skill, skimming in circles close to the balconies, and twittering as they darted by.

The arrival of this old gentleman changed essentially the aspect of affairs, but caused no jealousy nor collision. We tacitly shared the empire between us, like the last kings of Granada, excepting that we maintained a most amicable alliance. He reigned absolute over the Court of the Lions and its adjacent halls, while I maintained peaceful possession of the regions of the baths and the little garden of Lindaraxa. We took our meals together under the arcades of the court, where the fountains cooled the air, and bubbling rills ran along the channels of the marble pavement.

George Sand, quoted by Bayard Taylor in *The Atlantic*, 1867

I have never seen anything so bright, and at the same time so melancholy, as these perspectives where the ilex, the carob, pine, olive, poplar, and cypress mingle their various hues in the hollows of the mountain,– abysses of verdure, where the torrent precipitates its course under mounds of sumptuous richness and an inimitable grace. While you hear the sound of the sea on the northern coast, you perceive it only as a faint shining line beyond the sinking mountains of boldest outline, fringed with superb trees; and beyond these by rounded hills which the setting sun gilds with burning colours, where the eye distinguishes, a league away, the microscopic profile of trees, fine as the antennae of butterflies, black and clear as pencil drawings of Indian-ink on a ground of sparkling gold. It is one of those landscapes which oppress you, because they leave nothing to be desired, nothing to be imagined. Nature has here created that which the poet and the painter behold in their dreams. An immense *ensemble*, infinite details, inexhaustible variety, blended forms, sharp contours, dim vanishing depths, – are all present, and art can suggest nothing Further.

Majorca is one of the most beautiful countries of the world for the painter, and one of the least known. It is a green Helvetia under the sky of Calabria, with the solemnity and silence of the Orient.

Hilaire Belloc, *This and That and The Other*, 1912

This experience of Spain, this first discovery of a thing so unexpected and so universally misstated by the pens of travellers and historians, is best seen in autumn sunsets, I think, when behind the mass of the distant mountains an angry sky lights up its unfruitful aspect of desolation, and, though lending it a colour it can never possess in commoner hours and seasons, in no way creates an illusion of fertility or of romance, of yield or of adventure, in that doomed silence.

SWITZERLAND

Fyodor Dostoevsky, letter to his sister, January 1868

Geneva is a dull, gloomy, Protestant, stupid town with a frightful climate, but very well suited for work.

Mark Twain, *A Tramp Abroad*, 1880

We were approaching the renowned Matterhorn. A month before, this mountain had been only a name to us, but latterly we had been moving through a steadily thickening double row of pictures of it, done in oil, water, chromo, wood, steel, copper, crayon, and photography, and so it had at length become a shape to us – and a very distinct, decided, and familiar one, too. We were expecting to recognize that mountain whenever or wherever we should run across it. We were not deceived. The monarch was far away when we first saw him, but there was no such thing as mistaking him.

He has the rare peculiarity of standing by himself; he is peculiarly steep, too, and is also most oddly shaped. He towers into the sky like a colossal wedge, with the upper third of its blade bent a little to the left. The broad base of this monster wedge is planted upon a grand glacier-paved Alpine platform whose elevation is ten thousand feet above sea-level; as the wedge itself is some five thousand feet high, it follows that its apex is about fifteen thousand feet above sea-level. So the whole bulk of this stately piece of rock, this sky-cleaving monolith, is above the line of eternal snow. Yet while all its giant neighbors have the look of being built of solid snow, from their waists up, the Matterhorn stands black and naked and forbidding, the year round, or merely powdered or streaked with white in places, for its sides are so steep that the snow cannot stay there. Its strange form, its august isolation, and its majestic unkinship with its own kind, make it – so to speak – the Napoleon of the mountain world. 'Grand, gloomy, and peculiar,' is a phrase which fits it as aptly as it fitted the great captain.

Gerard Manley Hopkins, journal entry, July 1868

We went into the grotto and also the vault from which the Rhone flows. It looked like a blue tent and as you went further in changed to lilac. As you come out the daylight glazes the groins with gleaming rosecolour. The ice inside has a branchy wire texture. The man shewed us the odd way in which a little piece of ice will stick against the walls – as if drawn by a magnet.

Robert Louis Stevenson, *Essays of Travel*, 1905

A mountain valley has, at the best, a certain prison-like effect on the imagination, but a mountain valley, an Alpine winter, and an invalid's weakness make up among them a prison of the most effective kind. The roads indeed are cleared, and at least one footpath dodging up the hill; but to these the health-seeker is rigidly confined. There are for him no cross-cuts over the field, no following of streams, no unguided rambles in the wood. His walks are cut and dry. In five or six different directions he can push as far, and no farther, than his strength permits; never deviating from the line laid down for him and beholding at each repetition the same field of wood and snow from the same corner of the road. This, of itself, would be a little trying to the patience in the course of months; but to this is added, by the heaped mantle of the snow, an almost utter absence of detail and an almost unbroken identity of colour. Snow, it is true, is not merely white. The sun touches it with roseate and golden lights. Its own crushed infinity of crystals, its own richness of tiny sculpture, fills it, when regarded near at hand, with wonderful depths of coloured shadow, and, though wintrily transformed, it is still water, and has watery tones of blue. But, when all is said, these fields of white and blots of crude black forest are but a trite and staring substitute for the infinite variety and pleasantness of the earth's face. Even a boulder, whose front is too precipitous to have retained the snow, seems, if you come upon it in your walk, a perfect gem of colour, reminds you almost painfully of other places, and brings into your head the delights of more Arcadian days – the path across the meadow, the hazel dell, the lilies on the stream, and the scents, the colours, and the whisper of the woods. And scents here are as rare as colours. Unless you get a gust of kitchen in passing some hotel, you shall smell nothing all day long but the faint and choking odour of frost. Sounds, too, are absent: not a bird pipes, not a bough waves, in the dead, windless atmosphere. If a sleigh goes by, the sleigh-bells ring, and that is all; you work all winter through to no other accompaniment but the crunching of your steps upon the frozen snow.

It is the curse of the Alpine valleys to be each one village from one end to the other. Go where you please, houses will still be in sight, before and behind you, and to the right and left. Climb as high as an invalid is able, and it is only to spy new habitations nested in the wood. Nor is that all; for about the health resort the walks are besieged by single people walking rapidly with plaids about their shoulders, by sudden troops of German boys trying to learn to jodel, and by German couples silently and, as you venture to fancy, not quite happily, pursuing love's young dream. You may perhaps be an invalid who likes to make bad verses as he walks about. Alas! no muse will suffer this imminence of interruption – and at the second stampede of jodellers you find your modest inspiration fled. Or you may only have a taste for solitude; it may try your nerves to have some one always in front whom you are visibly overtaking, and some one always behind who is audibly overtaking you, to say nothing of a score or so who brush past you in an opposite direction. It may annoy you to take your walks and seats in public view. Alas! there is no help for it among the Alps. There are no recesses, as in Gorbio Valley by the oil-mill; no sacred solitude of olive gardens on the Roccabruna-road; no nook upon Saint Martin's Cape, haunted by the voice of breakers, and fragrant with the threefold sweetness of the rosemary and the sea-pines and the sea.

SCANDINAVIA

SWEDEN

Mary Wollstonecraft, *Letters Written During a Short Residence in Sweden, Norway and Denmark*, 1796

On entering, I was still better pleased to find a clean house, with some degree of rural elegance. The beds were of muslin, coarse it is true, but dazzlingly white; and the floor was strewed over with little sprigs of juniper (the custom, as I afterwards found, of the country), which formed a contrast with the curtains and produced an agreeable sensation of freshness, to soften the ardour of noon. Still nothing was so pleasing as the alacrity of hospitality – all that the house afforded was quickly spread on the whitest linen. – Remember I had just left the vessel, where, without being fastidious, I had continually been disgusted. Fish, milk, butter, and

cheese, and I am sorry to add, brandy, the bane of this country, were spread on the board. After we had dined, hospitality made them, with some degree of mystery, bring us some excellent coffee. I did not then know that it was prohibited.

The good man of the house apologized for coming in continually, but declared that he was so glad to speak English, he could not stay out, he need not have apologized; I was equally glad of his company. With the wife I could only exchange smiles; and she was employed observing the make of our clothes. My hands, I found, had first led her to discover that I was the lady. I had, of course, my quantum of reverences; for the politeness of the north seems to partake of the coldness of the climate, and the rigidity of its iron sinewed rocks. amongst the peasantry, there is, however, so much of the simplicity of the golden age in this land of flint – so much overflowing of heart, and fellow-feeling, that only benevolence, and the honest sympathy of nature, diffused smiles over my countenance when they kept me standing, regardless of my fatigue, whilst they dropt courtesy after courtesy.

The situation of this house was beautiful, though chosen for convenience. The master being the officer who commanded all the pilots on the coast, and the person appointed to guard wrecks, it was necessary for him to fix on a spot that would overlook the whole bay.

NORWAY

Mary Wollstonecraft, *Letters Written During a Short Residence in Sweden, Norway and Denmark*, 1796

As the Norwegians do not frequently see travellers, they are very curious to know their business, and who they are – so curious, that I was half tempted to adopt Dr. Franklin's plan, when travelling in America, where they are equally prying, which was to write on a paper, for public inspection, my name, from whence

EIN THEIL

SICKLAÖEN

HAMMERBY
SEE
Frisch
Waſſer

Hamerby

PARS

SVDERMÄNNZE

Rosenthal vague Bihas:

Waldemars Oen

Biſchofsweyken

Paſtorhauß

S:hams

Sudliens
Schiffswerst

HAMMERBY
SEE

Hamerby
Port

Syder-Port

Blockhausholm
mit dem Thurm und Kron:

Neu Schiffsholm

STOCKHOLM

SYDER

HORNS

Wycken

MALM

Riderholm
Ins:

A·ELLER
SEE

FROSCHE
See

AUStritt des

MAELLER SEE

INS:
LANGHOLM

MAELLER SEE

Raching
holm

LILLIE

HOLM

I came, where I was going, and what was my business. But if I were importuned by their curiosity, their friendly gestures gratified me. A woman coming alone interested them. And I know not whether my weariness gave me a look of peculiar delicacy, but they approached to assist me, and inquire after my wants, as if they were afraid to hurt, and wished to protect me.

* * *

It was late when I reached Tonsberg, and I was glad to go to bed at a decent inn. The next morning the 17th of July, conversing with the gentleman with whom I had business to transact, I found that I should be detained at Tonsberg three weeks, and I lamented that I had not brought my child with me.

The inn was quiet, and my room so pleasant, commanding a view of the sea, confined by an amphitheatre of hanging woods, that I wished to remain there, though no one in the house could speak English or French. The mayor, my friend, however, sent a young woman to me who spoke a little English, and she agreed to call on me twice a day to receive my orders and translate them to my hostess.

My not understanding the language was an excellent pretext for dining alone, which I prevailed on them to let me do at a late hour, for the early dinners in Sweden had entirely deranged my day. I could not alter it there without disturbing the economy of a family where I was as a visitor, necessity having forced me to accept of an invitation from a private family, the lodgings were so incommodious.

Amongst the Norwegians I had the arrangement of my own time, and I determined to regulate it in such a manner that I might enjoy as much of their sweet summer as I possibly could; short, it is true, but 'passing sweet.'

I never endured a winter in this rude clime, consequently it was not the contrast, but the real beauty of the season which made the present summer appear to me the finest I had ever seen. Sheltered from the north and eastern winds, nothing can exceed the salubrity, the soft freshness of the western gales. In the evening they also die away; the aspen leaves tremble into stillness, and reposing nature seems to be warmed by the moon, which here assumes a genial aspect. And if a light shower has chanced to fall with the sun, the juniper, the underwood of the forest, exhales a wild perfume, mixed with a thousand nameless sweets that, soothing the heart, leave images in the memory which the imagination will ever hold dear.

Roald Dahl, *Boy*, 1984

The next morning, everyone got up early and eager to continue the journey. There was another full day's travelling to be done before we reached our final destination, most of it by boat. We loved this part of our journey. The nice little vessel with its single tall funnel would move out into the calm waters of the fjord. Unless you have sailed down the Oslo fjord like this yourself on a lovely summer's day, you cannot imagine what it is like. It is impossible to describe the feeling of absolute peace and beauty that surrounds you. The boat winds its way between countless tiny islands, some with small brightly painted wooden houses on them, but many with not a house or a tree on the bare rocks.

Late in the afternoon, we would come finally to the end of the journey, the island of Fjome. This was where our mother always took us. Heaven knows how she found it, but to us it was the greatest place on earth.

North America

USA

Wilkie Collins, letter to Frederick Lehmann, written in Buffalo, New York, 2 January 1874

No matter where I go, my reception in America is always the same. The prominent people in each place visit me, drive me out, dine me, and do all that they can to make me feel myself among friends. The enthusiasm and kindness are really and truly beyond description. I should be the most ungrateful man living if I had any other than the highest opinion of the American people. I find them to be the most enthusiastic, the most cordial, and the most sincere people I have ever met with in my life. When an American says, 'Come and see me,' he <u>means</u> it. This is wonderful to an Englishman.

Before I had been a week in this country I noted three national peculiarities which had never been mentioned to me by visitors to the 'States.' I. No American hums or whistles a tune – either at home or on the street. II. Not one American in 500 has a dog. III. Not one American in a 1000 carries a walking stick. I, who hum perpetually – who love dogs – who cannot live without a walking stick – am greatly distressed at finding my dear Americans deficient in the three social virtues just enumerated.

Ian Fleming, *Thrilling Cities*, 1963

I enjoyed myself least of all in New York. It was my last lap and perhaps I was getting tired, but each time I come back (and I have revisited the city every year since the war) I feel that it has lost more of its heart. Steel and concrete, aluminium and copper sheathing for the new buildings, have smothered the brownstone streets that had so much warmth in the old days. The whole of the beautiful Washington Square area has disappeared, and up town the new resettlement areas – vast blocks of tiny apartments for the negroes and the Puerto Ricans – have now overwhelmed the old happy sprawl of Harlem.

There are still thrilling moments – when your taxi goes over the hump on Park Avenue at 69th Street and the lights turn to red and you pause and watch them all go green the whole way down to 46th, your heart turns over for New York. But this is an architectural, a physical, thrill. Go into the first drugstore, ask your way from a passer-by, and the indifference and harshness of the New Yorker cuts the old affection for the city out of your body as sharply as a surgeon's knife. It is partly the hysterical pursuit of money, the fast buck, that chills, but it is also the disdain of the New Yorker for the guy who doesn't know his way about, who isn't on the inside.

In New York you don't get politeness unless you pay for it. Here, the tipping system has gone mad. You are ruled by the head waiter, the bell captain, the reservation clerk, the credit manager and the black-market theatre-ticket operator. They are the Establishment, and you must be 'in' with these people or you will sink without trace. And, of course, in New York the expense-account aris-tocracy have increasingly ruined one's old haunts, deflating the quality of the food and inflating the prices.

Frances Trollope, *Domestic Manners of the Americans*, 1832

The gentlemen in the cabin (we had no ladies) would certainly neither, from their language, manners, nor appearance, have received that designation in Europe; but we soon found their claim to it rested on more substantial ground, for we heard them

nearly all addressed by the titles of general, colonel, and major. On mentioning these military dignities to an English friend some time afterwards, he told me that he too had made the voyage with the same description of company, but remarking that there was not a single captain among them; he made the observation to a fellow-passenger, and asked how he accounted for it. 'Oh, sir, the captains are all on deck,' was the reply.

...I know it is equally easy and invidious to ridicule the peculiarities of appearance and manner in people of a different nation from ourselves; we may, too, at the same moment, be undergoing the same ordeal in their estimation; and, moreover, I am by no means disposed to consider whatever is new to me as therefore objectionable; but, nevertheless, it was impossible not to feel repugnance to many of the novelties that now surrounded me.

The total want of all the usual courtesies of the table, the voracious rapidity with which the viands were seized and devoured, the strange uncouth phrases and pronunciation; the loathsome spitting, from the contamination of which it vas absolutely impossible to protect our dresses; the frightful manner of feeding with their knives, till the whole blade seemed to enter into the mouth; and the still more frightful manner of cleaning the teeth afterwards with a pocket knife, soon forced us to feel that we were not surrounded by the generals, colonels, and majors of the old world; and that the dinner hour was to be any thing rather than an hour of enjoyment.

Rupert Brooke, 'Niagara Falls', *Letters from America*, 1916

Beyond the foot of the Falls the river is like a slipping floor of marble, green with veins of dirty white, made by the scum that was foam. It slides very quietly and slowly down for a mile or two, sullenly exhausted. Then it turns to a dull sage green, and hurries more swiftly, smooth and ominous. As the walls of the ravine close in, trouble stirs, and the waters boil and eddy. These are the lower rapids, a sight more terrifying than the Falls, because less intelligible. Close in its bands of rock the river surges tumultuously forward, writhing and leaping as if inspired by a demon. It is pressed by the straits into a visibly convex form. Great planes of water slide past. Sometimes it is thrown up into a pinnacle of foam higher than a house, or leaps with incredible speed from the crest of one vast wave to another, along the shining curve between, like the spring of a wild beast. Its motion continually suggests muscular action. The power manifest in these rapids moves one with a different sense of awe and terror from that of the Falls. Here the inhuman life and strength are spontaneous, active, almost resolute; masculine vigor compared with the passive gigantic power, female, helpless and overwhelming, of the Falls. A place of fear.

One is drawn back, strangely, to a contemplation of the Falls, at every hour, and especially by night, when the cloud of spray becomes an immense visible ghost, straining and wavering high above the river, white and pathetic and translucent. The Victorian lies very close below the surface in every man. There one can sit and let great cloudy thoughts of destiny and the passage of empires drift through the mind; for such dreams are at home by Niagara. I could not get out of my mind the thought of a friend, who said that the rainbows over the Falls were like the arts and beauty and goodness, with regard to the stream of life – caused by it, thrown upon its spray, but unable to stay or direct or affect it, and ceasing when it ceased. In all comparisons that rise in the heart, the river, with its multitudinous waves and its single current, likens itself to a life, whether of an individual or of a community. A man's life is of many flashing moments, and yet one stream; a nation's flows through all its citizens, and yet is more than they. In such places, one is aware, with an almost insupportable and yet comforting certitude, that both men and nations are hurried onwards to their ruin or ending as inevitably as this dark flood. Some go down to it unreluctant, and meet it, like the river, not without nobility. And as incessant, as inevitable, and as unavailing as the spray that hangs over the Falls, is the white cloud of human crying….

Frances Kemble, *Journal*, 1835

I felt absolutely nervous with expectation. The sound of the cataract is, they say, heard within fifteen miles when the wind sets favourably: today, however, there was no wind; the whole air was breathless with the heat of midsummer, and, though we stopped our waggon once or twice to listen as we approached, all was profoundest silence. There was no motion in the leaves of the trees, not a cloud sailing in the sky; every thing was as though in a bright, warm death. When we were within about three miles of the Falls, just before entering the village of Niagara, ___stopped the waggon; and then we heard distinctly, though far off, the voice of the mighty cataract. Looking over the woods, which appeared to overhang the course of the river, we beheld one silver cloud rising slowly into the sky, – the everlasting incense of the waters. A perfect frenzy of impatience seized upon me: I could have set off and run the whole way; and when at length the carriage stopped at the door of the Niagara house, waiting neither for my father, D___, nor___, I rushed through the hall, and the garden, down the steep footpath cut in the rocks. I heard steps behind me; ___ was following me: down, down I sprang, and along the narrow footpath, divided only by a thicket from the tumultuous rapids. I saw through the boughs the white glimmer of that sea of foam. 'Go on, go on; don't stop,' shouted___, and in another minute the thicket was passed: I stood upon Table Rock ___seized me by the arm, and, without speaking a word, dragged me to the edge of the rapids, to the brink of the abyss. I saw Niagara. – Oh, God! who can describe that sight?

Charles Dickens, *American Notes*, 1843

I made acquaintance with an American railroad on this occasion, for the first time. As these works are pretty much alike all through the States, their general characteristics are easily described.

There are no first and second class carriages as with us; but there is a gentlemen's car and a ladies' car: the main distinction between which is, that in the first everybody smokes; and in the second, nobody does. As a black man never travels with a white one, there is also a negro car; which is a great, blundering, clumsy chest, such as Gulliver put to sea in from the kingdom of Brobdingnag. There is a great deal of jolting, a great deal of noise, a great deal of wall, not much window, a locomotive engine, a shriek, and a bell.

The cars are like shabby omnibuses, but larger: holding thirty, forty, fifty people. The seats, instead of stretching from end to end, are placed crosswise. Each seat holds two persons. There is a long row of them on each side of the caravan, a narrow passage up the middle, and a door at both ends. In the centre of the carriage there is usually a stove, fed with charcoal or anthracite coal; which is for the most part red-hot. It is insufferably close; and you see the hot air fluttering between yourself and any other object you may happen to look at, like the ghost of smoke.

In the ladies' car there are a great many gentlemen who have ladies with them. There are also a great many ladies who have nobody with them: for any lady may travel alone, from one end of the United States to the other, and be certain of the most courteous and considerate treatment everywhere. The conductor, or check-taker, or guard, or whatever he may be, wears no uniform. He walks up and down the car, and in and out of it, as his fancy dictates; leans against the door with his hands in his pockets, and stares at you, if you chance to be a stranger; or enters into conversation with the passengers about him. A great many newspapers are pulled out, and a few of them are read. Everybody talks to you, or to anybody else who hits his fancy. If you are an Englishman, he expects that that railroad is pretty much like an English railroad. If you say 'No,' he says 'Yes?' (interrogatively), and asks in what respect they differ. You enumerate the heads of difference, one by one, and he says 'Yes?' (still interrogatively) to each. Then he guesses that you don't travel faster in England; and on your replying that you do, says 'Yes?' again (still interrogatively), and, it is quite evident, don't believe it. After a long pause he remarks, partly to you, and partly to the knob on the top of his stick, that 'Yankees are reckoned to be considerable of a go-ahead people too;' upon which *you* say 'Yes,' and then *he* says 'Yes' again (affirmatively this time); and, upon your looking out of window, tells you that behind that hill, and some three miles from the next station, there is a clever town in a smart lo-ca-tion, where he expects you have concluded to stop. Your answer in the negative naturally

171

leads to more questions in reference to your intended route (always pronounced rout); and wherever you are going, you invariably learn that you can't get there without immense difficulty and danger, and that all the great sights are somewhere else.

If a lady take a fancy to any male passenger's seat, the gentleman who accompanies her gives him notice of the fact, and he immediately vacates it with great politeness. Politics are much discussed; so are banks, so is cotton. Quiet people avoid the question of the Presidency, for there will be a new election in three years and a half, and party feeling runs very high.

* * *

This narrow thoroughfare, baking and blistering in the sun, is Wall Street: the Stock Exchange and Lombard Street of New York. Many a rapid fortune has been made in this street, and many a no less rapid ruin. Some of these very merchants whom you see hanging about here now, have locked up money in their strong-boxes, like the man in the Arabian Nights, and opening them again, have found but withered leaves. Below, here by the water-side, where the bowsprits of ships stretch across the footway, and almost thrust themselves into the windows, lie the noble American vessels which have made their Packet Service the finest in the world. They have brought hither the foreigners who abound in all the streets: not, perhaps, that there are more here than in other commercial cities; but elsewhere they have particular haunts, and you must find them out; here they pervade the town.

We must cross Broadway again; gaining some refreshment from the heat in the sight of the great blocks of clean ice which are being carried into shops and bar-rooms; and the pine-apples and water-melons profusely displayed for sale. Fine streets of spacious houses here, you! – Wall Street has furnished and dismantled many of them very often – and here a deep green leafy square. Be sure that is a hospitable house, with inmates to be affectionately remembered always, where they have the open door and pretty show of plants within, and where the child with laughing eyes is peeping out of window at the little dog below. You wonder what may be the use of this tall flagstaff in the by-street, with something like Liberty's head-dress on its top: so do I. But there is a passion for tall flagstaffs hereabout, and you may see its twin brother in five minutes, if you have a mind.

Again across Broadway, and so – passing from the many-coloured crowd and glittering shops – into another long main street, the Bowery. A rail-road yonder, see, where two stout horses trot along, drawing a score or two of people and a great wooden ark with ease. The stores are poorer here, the passengers less gay. Clothes ready made, and meat ready cooked, are to be bought in these parts; and the lively whirl of carriages is exchanged for the deep rumble of carts and waggons. These signs which are so plentiful, in shape like river buoys, or small balloons, hoisted by cords to poles, and dangling there, announce, as you may see by looking up, 'OYSTERS IN EVERY STYLE.' They tempt the hungry most at night, for then dull candles, glimmering inside, illuminate these dainty words, and make the mouths of idlers water as they read and linger.

What is this dismal-fronted pile of bastard Egyptian, like an enchanter's palace in a melodrama? – A famous prison, called The Tombs.

* * *

Once more in Broadway! Here are the same ladies in bright colours, walking to and fro, in pairs and singly; yonder the very same light blue parasol which passed and repassed the hotel window twenty times while we were sitting there. We are going to cross here. Take care of the pigs. Two portly sows are trotting up behind this carriage, and a select party of half-a-dozen gentlemen hogs have just now turned the corner.

* * *

In this district, as in all others where slavery sits brooding (I have frequently heard this admitted, even by those who are its warmest advocates), there is an air of ruin and decay abroad, which is inseparable from the system. The barns and outhouses are mouldering away; the sheds are patched and half roofless; the log-cabins (built in Virginia with external chimneys made of clay or wood) are squalid in the last degree. There is no look of decent comfort anywhere. The miserable stations by the railway side; the great wild woodyards, whence the engine is supplied with fuel; the negro children rolling on the ground before the cabin doors, with dogs and pigs; the biped beasts of burden slinking past: gloom and dejection are upon them all.

* * *

Cincinnati is a beautiful city; cheerful, thriving, and animated. I have not often seen a place that commends itself so favourably and pleasantly to a stranger at the first glance as this does: with its clean houses of red and white, its well-paved roads, and footways bright tile. Nor does it become less prepossessing on a closer acquaintance. The streets are broad and airy, the shops extremely good, the private residences remarkable for their elegance and neatness. There is something of invention and fancy in the varying styles of these latter erections, which, after the dull company of the steamboat, is perfectly delightful, as conveying an assurance that there are such qualities still in existence. The disposition to ornament these pretty villas, and render them attractive, leads to the culture of trees and flowers, and the laying out of well-kept gardens, the sight of which, to those who walk along the streets, is inexpressibly refreshing and agreeable. I was quite charmed with the appearance of the town, and its adjoining suburb of Mount Auburn; from which the city, lying in an amphitheatre of hills, forms a picture of remarkable beauty, and is seen to great advantage.

There happened to be a great Temperance Convention held here on the day after our arrival; and as the order of march brought the procession under the windows of the hotel in which we lodged, when they started in the morning, I had a good opportunity of seeing it. It comprised several thousand men; the members of various 'Washington Auxiliary Temperance Societies;' and was marshalled by officers on horseback, who cantered briskly up and down the line, with scarfs and ribbons of bright colours fluttering out behind them gaily. There were bands of music, too, and banners out of number: and it was a fresh, holiday-looking concourse altogether.

Elinor Mordaunt, *Purely for Pleasure*, 1932

The drive from San Antonio has been a scorching experience, through clouds of dust. The moment I get up to my room I start unpacking, searching for clean clothes; turn on my bath. And here in the Texan wilds, in this raw commercial town, every bedroom in the hotel boasts its own bathroom, its own telephone – though at the same time there is a notice hung upon the wall: 'Gentlemen are requested not to wipe their boots on the face towels, or lie on the bed in their spurs.'

WAKE ISLAND

Ian Fleming, *Thrilling Cities*, 1963

Wake Island, which is an important aircraft staging-point, is notable for having absolutely no air-conditioning. I had always assumed that the first civilizing benefits Americans brought to newly acquired overseas territories were Coca-Cola, corned beef hash, and canned air, in that order. It was about ninety-five degrees in the mosquito-netted Quonsett huts that are the only buildings on Wake, and we spent an exhausting day nodding enthusiastically as successive ground and crew personnel came up and assured us how lucky we had been, Bud. Wake is one of the homes of the Pacific albatross, now so much disturbed, I believe, by the aircraft that they are in danger of extermination, but it was too hot to go and visit their haunts in the mangroves at the other end of the island. Instead, I slept gratefully in the spare crew quarters and gossiped with a man with a spotted dog who was in charge of quarantined animals – mostly monkeys and parrots en route for the States after being collected in the East by tourists. He told me that, though he liked life on Wake, there was nothing to do there but skin-dive and teach parrots in transit dirty words to shock their American owners.

HAWAII

Ian Fleming, *Thrilling Cities*, 1963

Back in my hotel bedroom, I looked out at the sea which lay like gunmetal under a crescent moon. One or two night surfriders were still at it on the darkened creaming waves. Far below me, on the moon-burnt beach, an elderly woman, probably a General Electric cashier, was holding up her muumuu while the small waves washed her feet. She looked forlorn and unloved in this place of the eternal honeymoon. The next day, probably, she would be back in Seattle, Iowa, New Orleans. Now, in the path of the moon and with the gay flambeaux and the crooning guitars behind her, she was having her last paddle. She seemed to represent the tragedy of all ended holidays.

CANADA

H. Hesketh Prichard, *Through Trackless Labrador*, 1911

It is a wonderful place, this roof of the Labrador. Ridge on ridge, some of considerable height, roll away seemingly to the world's end. In the valleys and cups of the hills lie thousands of nameless lakes. The winds, during the greater part of the year, rage over it. It is sheer desolation, abysmal and chaotic. Of dominant notes there are but two, the ivory-coloured reindeer moss and the dark Laurentian stone. On the flanks and on the peaks of the mountains, in the beds of the brooks, on the shore of the lakes all over this huge tableland, are strewn the grey Laurentian boulders in their infinite millions gigantic and glacier-born seeds sown in the dawning of the world. When the sun shines, to quote Saltatha, the Yellowknife Indian, 'the lakes are sometimes misty, and sometimes blue, and the loons cry very often.' Then it is a land of stern and imposing beauty, perhaps unlike any other on earth, where sky and clouds are mirrored in the shallow lakes, and the lazy, monster fish rise among the ripples in the red and gold of evening. But when the clouds ride it, and the wind and rain, sleet and snow rave over it, as they do nearly all the year round, a desolation more appalling cannot be conceived.

CENTRAL AMERICA, SOUTH AMERICA, THE CARIBBEAN

ARGENTINA

Gerald Durrell, *Encounters with Animals*, 1958

I am constantly being surprised by the number of people, in different parts of the world, who seem to be quite oblivious to the animal life around them. To them the tropical forests or the savannah or the mountains in which they live are apparently devoid of life. All they see is a sterile landscape. This was brought home most forcibly to me when I was in Argentina. In Buenos Aires I met a man, an Englishman who had spent his whole life in Argentina, and when he learnt that my wife and I intended to go out into the pampa to look for animals he stared at us in genuine astonishment.

'But, my dear chap, you won't find anything *there*,' he exclaimed.

'Why not?' I inquired, rather puzzled, for he seemed an intelligent person.

'But the pampa is just a lot of grass,' he explained, waving his arms wildly in an attempt to show the extent of the grass, 'nothing, my dear fellow, absolutely nothing but grass punctuated by cows.'

Now, as a rough description of the pampa this is not so very wide of the mark except that life on this vast plain does not consist entirely of cows and gauchos. Standing in the pampa you can turn slowly round and on all sides of you, stretching away to the horizon, the grass lies flat as a billiard-table, broken here and there by the clumps of giant thistles, six or seven feet high, like some extraordinary surrealist candelabra. Under the hot blue sky it does seem to be a dead landscape, but under the shimmering cloak of grass, and in the small forests of dry, brittle thistle-stalks the amount of life is extraordinary. During the hot part of the day, riding on horseback across the thick carpet of grass, or pushing through a giant thistle-forest so that the brittle stems cracked and rattled like fireworks, there was little to be seen except the birds. Every forty or fifty yards there would be burrowing owls, perched straight as guardsmen on a tussock of grass near their holes, regarding you with astonished frosty-cold eyes, and, when you got close, doing a little bobbing dance of anxiety before taking off and wheeling over the grass on silent wings.

Inevitably your progress would be observed and reported on by the watchdogs of the pampa, the black-and-white spur-winged plovers, who would run furtively to and fro, ducking their heads and watching you carefully, eventually taking off and swooping round and round you on piebald wings, screaming 'Tero-tero-tero … tero … tero,' the alarm cry that warned everything for miles around of your presence. Once this strident warning had been given, other plovers in the distance would take it up, until it seemed as though the whole pampa rang with their cries. Every living thing was now alert and suspicious. Ahead, from the skeleton of a dead tree, what appeared to be two dead branches would suddenly take wing and soar up into the hot blue sky: chimango hawks with handsome rust-and-white plumage and long slender legs. What you had thought was merely an extra-large tussock of sun-dried grass would suddenly hoist itself up on to long stout legs and speed away across the grass in great loping strides, neck stretched out, dodging and twisting between the thistles, and you realized that your grass tussock had been a rhea, crouching low in the hope that you would pass it by. So, while the plovers were a nuisance in advertising your advance, they helped to panic the other inhabitants of the pampa into showing themselves.

Occasionally you would come across a 'laguana', a small shallow lake fringed with reeds and a few stunted trees. Here there were fat green frogs, but frogs which, if molested, jumped *at* you with open mouth, uttering fearsome gurking noises. In pursuit of the frogs were slender snakes marked in grey, black and vermilion red, like old school ties, slithering through the grass. In the rushes you would be almost sure to find the nest of a screamer, a bird like a great grey turkey: the youngster crouching in the slight depression in the sun-baked ground, yellow as a buttercup, but keeping absolutely still even when your horse's legs straddled it, while its parents paced frantically about, giving plaintive trumpeting cries of anxiety, intermixed with softer instructions to their chick.

This was the pampa during the day. In the evening, as you rode homeward, the sun was setting in a blaze of coloured clouds, and on the laguanas various ducks were flighting in, arrowing the smooth water with ripples as they landed. Small flocks of spoonbills drifted down like pink clouds to feed in the shallows among snowdrifts of black-necked swans.

As you rode among the thistles and it grew darker you might meet armadillos, hunched and intent, trotting like strange mechanical toys on their nightly scavenging; or perhaps a skunk who would stand, gleaming vividly black and white in the twilight, holding his tail stiffly erect while he stamped his front feet in petulant warning.

This, then, was what I saw of the pampa in the first few days. My friend had lived in Argentina all his life and had never realized that this small world of birds and animals existed. To him the pampa was 'nothing but grass punctuated by cows'. I felt sorry for him.

Novissima et Accuratissima
TOTIUS
AMERICÆ
DESCRIPTIO,
per
N. VISSCHER.

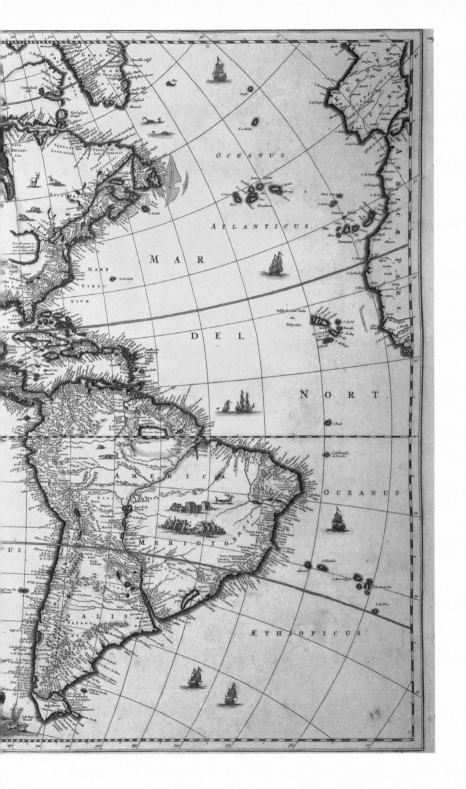

BERMUDA

Andrew Marvell, 'Bermudas', 1654

Where the remote Bermudas ride
In th' ocean's bosom unespy'd,
From a small boat, that row'd along,
The list'ning winds receiv'd this song.

What should we do but sing his praise
That led us through the wat'ry maze
Unto an isle so long unknown,
And yet far kinder than our own?
Where he the huge sea-monsters wracks,
That lift the deep upon their backs,
He lands us on a grassy stage,
Safe from the storm's and prelates' rage.
He gave us this eternal spring
Which here enamels everything,
And sends the fowls to us in care,
On daily visits through the air.
He hangs in shades the orange bright,
Like golden lamps in a green night;
And does in the pomegranates close
Jewels more rich than Ormus shows.
He makes the figs our mouths to meet
And throws the melons at our feet,
But apples plants of such a price,
No tree could ever bear them twice.
With cedars, chosen by his hand,
From Lebanon, he stores the land,
And makes the hollow seas that roar

Proclaim the ambergris on shore.
He cast (of which we rather boast)
The Gospel's pearl upon our coast,
And in these rocks for us did frame
A temple, where to sound his name.
Oh let our voice his praise exalt,
Till it arrive at heaven's vault;
Which thence (perhaps) rebounding, may
Echo beyond the Mexic Bay.

Thus sung they in the English boat
An holy and a cheerful note,
And all the way, to guide their chime,
With falling oars they kept the time.

BRAZIL

Sir Richard Burton, *Wanderings in Three Continents*, 1901

As evening approached the weather waxed cool and clear, and the excessive evaporation gave the idea of great dryness; my books curled up, it was hardly possible to write, and it reminded me of the Persian Gulf, where water-colours cannot be used because the moisture is absorbed from the brush.

The first view of Santa Lusia was very pleasing; a tall ridge about a mile from the stream was capped with two double-towered churches, divided by fine, large, whitewashed houses and rich vegetation, with palms straggling down to the water. Here I landed and made my way to the hotel, which was a most tumble-down hole, and after supper inspected Santa Lusia. It was formerly a centre of the gold diggings, but at this time possessed nothing of interest.

The next morning was delicious, and the face of Nature was

as calm as if it could show no other expression. The sword-like rays of the sun, radiating from the unseen centre before it arose in its splendour, soon dispersed the thin mists that slept tranquilly upon the cool river-bed. We shot the Ponte Grande de Santa Lusia to Cruvello and the backwoods. The bridge was the usual long, crooked affair, with twelve trusses, or trestles, in the water and many outside, showing that the floods are here extensive. The girders are rarely raised high enough, and an exceptional inundation sweeps them away, leaving bare poles bristling in the bed and dangerous piles under water.

About two miles below Santa Lusia the water became deeper and the country changed. The right, or eastern, side was rough and hilly, with heights hugging the bed. Near the other bank the land was more level, and the soil showed a better complexion, by which both sugar-cane and timber profited. In another hour we sighted the first cotton plantation, and right well it looked. There was indeed a mine of neglected wealth in cotton and fish along, and in, this river, and the more I saw of it the richer I found it. The hills were clothed with thin brown-grey grass, looking in places as if they were frosty with hoar, and always profusely tasselled.

CHILE

W.H. Hudson, *Idle Days in Patagonia*, 1893

On arriving at a hill, I would slowly ride to its summit, and stand there to survey the prospect. On every side it stretched away in great undulations; but the undulations were wild and irregular; the hills were rounded and cone-shaped, they were solitary and in groups and ranges; some sloped gently, others were ridge-like and stretched away in league-long terraces, with other terraces beyond; and all alike were clothed in the grey everlasting thorny vegetation. How grey it all was! hardly less so near at hand than on the haze-wrapped horizon, where the hills were dim and the outline blurred by distance. Sometimes I would see the large eagle-like, white-breasted buzzard, 'Buteo erythronotus', perched on the summit of a bush half a mile away; and so long as it would continue stationed motionless before me my eyes would remain involuntarily fixed on it, just as one keeps his eyes on a bright light shining in the gloom; for the whiteness of the hawk seemed to exercise a fascinating power on the vision, so surpassingly bright was it by contrast in the midst of that universal unrelieved greyness. Descending from my look-out, I would take up my aimless wanderings again, and visit other elevations to gaze on the same landscape from another point; and so on for hours, and at noon I would dismount and sit or lie on my folded poncho for an hour or longer.

Charles Darwin, *Voyage of the Beagle*, 1839

Under the diminished pressure, of course water boils at a lower temperature; in consequence of this the potatoes after boiling for some hours were as hard as ever; the pot was left on the fire all night, but yet the potatoes were not softened. I found out this, by overhearing in the morning my companions discussing the cause; they came to the simple conclusion that 'the cursed pot (which was a new one) did not choose to boil potatoes'.

CUBA

Amelia Murray, *Letters from the United States, Cuba and Canada*, 1856

We left Havana by the six o clock train the day before yesterday; reached Guines by nine; went to see a cave in a chalky hill three miles from the village – a fatiguing and difficult expedition, but I found numerous flowers known in our gardens and hot-houses; among them the pretty Asclepias tuberosa, Ipomceas of all colours and sizes, a lilac scilla, a solamena, and other things new to me, and the whole country was dotted over by cocoa-nut trees. That neighbourhood has little other foliage, although during our journey by rail I saw fine mango and other trees – among them a palmetto as tall as the Charmerops of Florida; it looks some

thing like the same species. We passed many haciendas, the plantations belonging to which were in high cultivation, great herds of cattle and many horses feeding about them; and there were tall chimneys indicating steam-engines for crushing sugar.

Christopher Columbus, *Journal of the First Voyage*, 1492

If the others already seen are very beautiful, green, and fertile, this is much more so, with large trees and very green. Here there are large lagoons with wonderful vegetation on their banks. Throughout the island all is green, and the herbage like April in Andalusia. The songs of the birds were so pleasant that it seemed as if a man could never wish to leave the place. The flocks of parrots concealed the sun; and the birds were so numerous, and of so many different kinds, that it was wonderful. There are trees of a thousand sorts, and all have their several fruits; and I feel the most unhappy man in the world not to know them, for I am well assured that they are all valuable. I bring home specimens of them, and also of the land. Thus walking along round one of the lakes I saw a serpent, which we killed, and I bring home the skin for your Highnesses. As soon as it saw us it went into the lagoon, and we followed, as the water was not very deep, until we killed it with lances. It is 7 spans long, and I believe that there are many like it in these lagoons. Here I came upon some aloes, and I have determined to take ten quintals on board to-morrow, for they tell me that they are worth a good deal. Also, while in search of good water, we came to a village about half a league from our anchorage. The people, as soon as they heard us, all fled and left their houses, hiding their property in the wood. I would not allow a thing to be touched, even the value of a pin. Presently some men among them came to us, and one came quite close. I gave him some bells and glass beads, which made him very content and happy. That our friendship might be further increased, I resolved to ask him for something; I requested him to get some water. After I had gone on board, the natives came to the beach with calabashes full of water, and they delighted much in giving it to us. I ordered another string of glass beads to be presented to them, and they said they would come again tomorrow.

JAMAICA

Aldous Huxley, *Beyond the Mexique Bay*, 1949

Jamaica is the Pearl of the Caribbean – or is it the Clapham Junction of the West ? I can never remember. But, anyhow, pearl or junction, it made us both feel extremely ill, and we were thankful to be off on a small Norwegian banana boat, bound for British Honduras and Guatemala.

Hans Sloane, *A Voyage to the Islands Madera, Barbados, Nievas, S. Christophers and Jamaica...*, 1707

Pelicans fish in this bay, likewise in blowing weather, when they cannot fish abroad, and in the calm mornings they dive after their prey. Spanish mackerel are taken in this bay in plenty. They are like ours, only made like a bonito. I here observed a small shoal of small fishes to leap out of the water, being pursued by greater fishes.

The whole shoals between Port Royal and Passage-Fort are covered with coral of several sorts, and *Alga angustifolia vitrariorum* or sea-grass. There are also star-fishes of several sorts, large and five-pointed, as well as small, and several sorts of the *Echinus marmus*. Alligators are often drawn on shore in the seine-nets by the fishermen, whose nets are generally broken by them. These alligators are so called from the word *alagarta*, in Spanish, signifying a lizard, of which this is an amphibious sort. When I was in

Jamaica there was one of these used to do abundance of mischief to the people's cattle in the neighborhood of this bay, having his regular courses to look for prey. One of the inhabitants there, as I was told, tied a long cord to his bedstead, and to the other end of the cord fastened a piece of wood and a dog, so that the alligator swallowing the dog and piece of wood, the latter came cross his throat, as it was designed, and after pulling the bedstead to the window, and awaking the person in bed, he was caught. Alligators love dogs extremely, but prey also on cattle. This alligator was nineteen feet long.

MEXICO

D. H. Lawrence, *Mornings in Mexico*, 1927

It is morning, and it is Mexico. The sun shines. But then, during the winter, it always shines. It is pleasant to sit out of doors and write, just fresh enough and just warm enough. But then it is Christmas next week, so it ought to be just right.

There is a little smell of carnations, because they are the nearest thing. And there is a resinous smell of ocote wood, and a smell of coffee, and a faint smell of leaves, and of Morning, and even of Mexico. Because when all is said and done, Mexico has a faint, physical scent of her own, as each human being has. And this is a curious, inexplicable scent, in which there are resin and perspiration and sunburned earth and urine among other things.

And cocks are still crowing. The little mill where the natives have their own corn ground is puffing rather languidly. And because some women are talking in the entrance-way, the two tame parrots in the trees have started to whistle.

The parrots, even when I don't listen to them, have an extraordinary effect on me. They make my diaphragm convulse with little laughs, almost mechanically. They are a quite commonplace pair of green birds, with bits of bluey red, and round, disillusioned eyes, and heavy, overhanging noses. But they listen intently. And they reproduce. The pair whistle now like Rosalino, who is sweeping the *patio* with a twig broom; and yet it is so unlike him, to be whistling full vent, when any of us is around, that one looks at him to see. And the moment one sees him, with his black head bent rather drooping and hidden as he sweeps, one laughs.

The parrots whistle exactly like Rosalino, only a little more so. And this little-more-so is extremely sardonically funny. With their sad old long-jowled faces and their flat disillusioned eyes, they reproduce Rosalino and a little-more-so without moving a muscle. And Rosalino, sweeping the *patio* with his twig broom,

scraping and tittering leaves into little heaps, covers himself more and more with the cloud of his own obscurity. He doesn't rebel. He is powerless. Up goes the wild, sliding Indian whistle into the morning, very powerful, with an immense energy seeming to drive behind it. And always, always a little more than life-like.

THE POLES

THE POLES

Antonio Pigafetta, *Journal of Magellan's Voyage*, c. 1525

Then proceeding on the same course toward the Antarctic Pole, coasting along the land, we came to anchor at two islands full of geese and sea-wolves. Truly, the great number of those geese cannot be reckoned; in one hour we loaded the five ships [with them]. Those geese are black and have all their feathers alike both on body and wings. They do not fly, and live on fish. They were so fat that it was not necessary to pluck them but to skin them. Their beak is like that of a crow. Those sea-wolves are of various colors, and as large as a calf, with a head like that of a calf, ears small and round, and large teeth. They have no legs but only feet with small nails attached to the body, which resemble our hands, and between their fingers the same kind of skin as the geese. They would be very fierce if they could run. They swim, and live on fish. At that place the ships suffered a very great storm, during which the three holy bodies appeared to us many times, that is to say, St. Elmo, St. Nicholas, and St. Clara, whereupon the storm quickly ceased.

Sir Ernest Shackleton, *South! The Story of Shackleton's Last Expedition 1914–1917*, 1919

We said good-bye to the sun on May 1 and entered the period of twilight that would be followed by the darkness of midwinter. The sun by the aid of refraction just cleared the horizon at noon and set shortly before 2 p.m. A fine aurora in the evening was

dimmed by the full moon, which had risen on April 27 and would not set again until May 6. The disappearance of the sun is apt to be a depressing event in the polar regions, where the long months of darkness involve mental as well as physical strain. But the *Endurance's* company refused to abandon their customary cheerfulness, and a concert in the evening made the Ritz a scene of noisy merriment, in strange contrast with the cold, silent world that lay outside.

'One feels our helplessness as the long winter night closes upon us. By this time, if fortune had smiled upon the Expedition, we would have been comfortably and securely established in a shore base, with depots laid to the south and plans made for the long march in the spring and summer. Where will we make a landing now? It is not easy to forecast the future. The ice may open in the spring, but by that time we will be far to the north-west. I do not think we shall be able to work back to Vahsel Bay. There are

possible landing-places on the western coast of the Weddell Sea, but can we reach any suitable spot early enough to attempt the overland journey next year? Time alone will tell. I do not think any member of the Expedition is disheartened by our disappointment. All hands are cheery and busy, and will do their best when the time for action comes. In the meantime we must wait.'

Agatha Christie, *An Autobiography*, 1977

From South Africa we set sail for Australia. It was a long, rather grey voyage. It was a mystery to me why, as the Captain explained, the shortest way to Australia was to go down towards the Pole and up again. He drew diagrams which eventually convinced me, but it is difficult to remember that the earth is round and has flat poles. It is a geographical fact, but not one that you appreciate the point of in real life. There was not much sunshine, but it was a fairly calm and pleasant voyage.

AUSTRALASIA

AUSTRALIA

William Dampier, *A New Voyage Round the World*, 1697

New Holland is a very large Tract of Land. It is not yet determined whether it is an Island or a main Continent, but I am certain that it joins neither to Asia, Africa nor America. The part of it that we saw is all low, even Land with sandy Banks against the Sea. Only the Points are rocky, and so are some of the Islands in this Bay.

The Land is of a dry sandy Soil, destitute of water except you make Wells, yet producing diverse sorts of Trees. But the Woods are not thick, nor the Trees very big. Most of the Trees that we saw are Dragon-Trees as we supposed, and these too are the largest Trees of any there. They are about the bigness of our large Apple-trees and about the same height, and the Rind is blackish and somewhat rough. The Leaves are of a dark Colour. Gum distils out of the Knots or Cracks that are in the Bodies of the Trees. We compared it with some Gum-Dragon, or Dragon's Blood, that was aboard, and it was of the same colour and taste. The other sorts of Tree were not known by any of us. There was pretty long Grass growing under the Trees but it was very thin. We saw no Trees that bore Fruit or Berries.

We saw no sort of Animal, nor any Tracks of Beasts but once, and that seemed to be the Tread of a Beast as big as a great Mastiff Dog. There are a few small Land-birds, but none bigger than a Blackbird, and but few Sea-fowls. Nor is the Sea very plentifully stored with Fish unless you reckon the Manatee and Turtle as such. Of these Creatures there is plenty, but they are extraordinarily shy, though the Inhabitants cannot trouble them much, having neither Boats nor Iron.

Sir Joseph Banks, *The Endeavour Journal of Sir Joseph Banks*, 1770

1770 June 25

In gathering plants today I myself had the good fortune to see the beast so much talkd of, tho but imperfectly; he was not only like a grey hound in size and running but had a long tail, as long as any grey hounds; what to liken him to I could not tell, nothing certainly that I have seen at all resembles him.

Captain James Cook, *Journal*, 1773

From what I have said of the Natives of New-Holland they may appear to some to be the most wretched people upon Earth, but in reality they are far more happier than we Europeans; being wholly unacquainted not only with the superfluous but the necessary Conveniences so much sought after in Europe, they are happy in not knowing the use of them. They live in a Tranquillity which is not disturb'd by the Inequality of Condition: The Earth and sea of their own accord furnishes them with all things necessary for life, they covet not Magnificent Houses, Household-stuff &c., they live in a warm and fine Climate and enjoy a very wholesome Air…. In short they seem'd to set no Value upon any thing we gave them, nor would they ever part with any thing of their own for any one article we could offer them; this in my opinion argues that they think themselves provided with all the necessarys of Life and that they have no superfluities.

Joseph Conrad, *Mirror of the Sea*, 1906

Sydney, where, from the heart of the fair city, down the vista of important streets, could be seen the wool-clippers lying at the

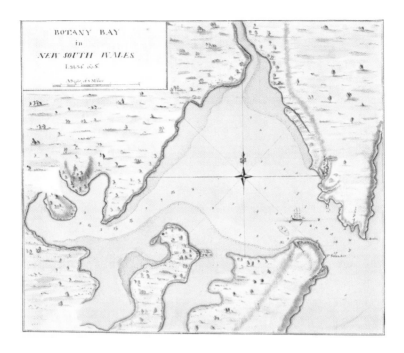

Circular Quay – no walled prison-house of a dock that, but the integral part of one of the finest, most beautiful, vast, and safe bays the sun ever shone upon. Now great steam-liners lie at these berths, always reserved for the sea aristocracy – grand and imposing enough ships, but here to-day and gone next week; whereas the general cargo, emigrant, and passenger clippers of my time, rigged with heavy spars, and built on fine lines, used to remain for months together waiting for their load of wool. Their names attained the dignity of household words. On Sundays and holidays the citizens trooped down, on visiting bent, and the lonely officer on duty solaced himself by playing the cicerone – especially to the citizenesses with engaging manners and a well-developed sense of the fun that may be got out of the inspection of a ship's cabins and state-rooms. The tinkle of more or less untuned cottage pianos floated out of open stern-ports till the gas-lamps began

EAST INDIA ISLES & AUSTRALIA.

British Statute Miles.
100 200 300 400 500

Ladrone or Marian
Anatajan Tinian
Guaham Saypan Birds I.
Islands

Egoy Isles Farroilep Feis
Yap Tosorow Pais
Sorol Derockoop Oroloc
Phillip Is. 1791 Lotook Howets I.
Thirteen I. Two I. Fais
Poulon Magoraves I. Young Williams I.

Pegadet or Torres I.
Schooq Koop
Lamoel
Raven I.

THE CAROLINE ISLANDS

Equator

Pitt I.
Fire Pt. Scarboro's Range
Cooks I. Marshalls I.
Balls I. Simpsons I.

Chasma I. Durours I. Mathias I. Kyne I.
Medios I. Admiralty I. Vickers I.
Church Mt. Dampieorsiro. Scooters I.
New Ireland High I.
St. Johns, Cocoa I.

SOUTH

Blasays I. Groupe
Kingsmith Ferens I.
Drummonds I.
Hards I.

OR NEW GUINEA
Volcano

SEA New Britain
SOLOMONS Arch
Bristons I. St.
Torres des Arsacides
Mannings I.

Kennedy's I.
Stewarts I.
Malanta Lobes
Duff Group

Taswells I.
Thereons I.

Torres
Strait
Rock I.
Sir C. Hardys Pt.
Weymouth
Longsiede

Bennells I.
C. Delaverance

Tucopia
Mitre I.
Cherry I.

Rotumah

Gulf of
Carpentaria
Peral I.
Sir E. Pellews
Sir E. Pellew I.

Q. Charlottes Arch
Torres Pt.
Banter I.

Australia del Espiritu
Santo Aurora I.
Whitsuntide I.
Mallicollo

C. Platjory
C. Grafton Green I.
Pit Roy I.
Double Pt.
Halifax B.
C. Gloucester
Hamptons Pt.
Moulon I.

PACIFIC

NEW HEBUDEN
Errooma
Tanna I.
Immer

Vutoree
Tackonoroa
Sidney
Ambow
Isles
Mywoulla

North I.

NEW CALEDONIA
South C.
Walpole I.

NEW

Cumberland I.
Northumberland I.
Townsend I.
Keppel Bay
Keppel I.
Bustard B.

LIA
SOUTH

C. Capricorn
Herveys B.
Sandy Cape

Norfolk I.
Philip I.

Glasshouse B. Morton I.
L. Danger

WALES

Smoaky C.
C. Hawke
Port Stephens
Sidney Port Jackson
Botany Bay
Jervis Bay
Montague I.
C. Howe

Ld. Howes I.

OCEAN

Flinders Roos
T. Riley
G. St. Vincent
C. Jervis
Bernouilli

Victoria

Wilsons Prom
Western Port
Port Philip
Ram Head

C. Maria Van Diemen
North C.
C. Brett
Gabrille
Plenty B.

NEW

Kings I. Furneaux I.
Bridgewater
Hunters I.
Kings I.
Bass's Strait
Banks's Strait

Gunnet I.
C. Egmont
C. Farewell
Cooks Strait

C. East
Poverty B.
Hawks B.
Castle Pt.
C. Palliser

YAN DIEMENS
LAND
Puramid
Hobart
S. W. C.
C. Pillar
Fred. Henry B.
St. Patricks Hd.

ZEA
Cascade Pt.
TAVAI POEN-AMOO
Doubtful Harb.
West C.
S. W. Bay

LAND
Campbell
Banks's I.
C. Saunders
S. E. Bay

to twinkle in the streets, and the ship's night-watchman, coming sleepily on duty after his unsatisfactory day slumbers, hauled down the flags and fastened a lighted lantern at the break of the gangway. The night closed rapidly upon the silent ships with their crews on shore. Up a short, steep ascent by the King's Head pub, patronized by the cooks and stewards of the fleet, the voice of a man crying 'Hot saveloys!' at the end of George Street, where the cheap eating-houses (sixpence a meal) were kept by Chinamen (Sun-kum-on's was not bad), is heard at regular intervals.

Joshua Slocum, *Sailing Alone Around the World*, 1899

The Pacific is perhaps, upon the whole, no more boisterous than other oceans, though I feel quite safe in saying that it is not more pacific except in name. It is often wild enough in one part or another. I once knew a writer who, after saying beautiful things about the sea, passed through a Pacific hurricane, and he became a changed man. But where, after all, would be the poetry of the sea were there no wild waves? At last here was the *Spray* in the midst of a sea of coral. The sea itself might be called smooth indeed, but coral rocks are always rough, sharp, and dangerous. I trusted now to the mercies of the Maker of all reefs, keeping a good lookout at the same time for perils on every hand.

Lo! the Barrier Reef and the waters of many colours studded all about with enchanted islands!

Sydney Parkinson, *A Journal of a Voyage to the South Seas, in His Majesty's Ship: The Endeavour*, 1773

This bay is in latitude 34°6', and makes a good harbour, being only two or three points open to the eastward; but the water is in general shallow; and it has several arms extending from it, which are also shallow. On these shallows we found a great number of rays, some shell-fish, and a few sharks. The rays are

of an enormous size: one of them which we caught weighed two hundred and thirty-nine pounds, and another three hundred and twenty-six. They tasted very much like the European rays, and the viscera had an agreeable flavour, not unlike stewed turtle. These rays, and shell-fish, are the natives chief food.

Marianne North, *Recollections of a Happy Life*, 1893

But it was always raining in this unexpected bit of the tropics, and I had no easy task to finish a picture there. Three times I packed up my things in disgust, and at last brought home my paper wetter with rain than with oil paint. People were all related to one another, and all hospitable, and I drove from house to house only regretting that the horse and buggy were not my own, when I could have stayed much longer with enjoyment. Another day I stopped to paint a gigantic fig tree standing alone, its huge buttresses covered with tangled creepers and parasites. The village was called Figtree Village after it, and all the population was on horseback, going to the races at Wollongong.

At Mr. H. O.'s I saw a grand specimen of the red cedar. It had leaves like the ailanthus, but its wood smelt like cedar pencils and was red as mahogany, which gave it its name. The tea trees there were covered with tiny white bottlebrush flowers and were rosy with their young shoots and leaves. Another sort was called the paperbark tree (*Melaleuca* sp.) One could pull lumps of soft paper from it, tear it apart, and write on it without difficulty in a blotty sort of way. There were some old dead gum trees left standing near the house to show the steps cut in them by opossum-hunting natives, who now no longer existed in those parts. The notches were probably only cut big enough to rest the great toe in, but the bark and tree had swelled as it grew older, and the holes were now large enough to hold the whole foot. Some of them had been enlarged into nests by the laughing jackass. Lots of those comical birds perched on those trees and gossiped about us as we sat and watched them.

The garden at Doondale was a sight to see: pink and white *Azalea indica* fit for London shows, bougainvillea with three yellow blooms at once in their purple bracts, flame trees (*Sterculia* sp.), gorgeous Cape lilies, and all our home flowers in perfection. I was offered the loan of this lovely house for a month when they were all going to another house on the cooler side of the hills. It had a valley of ferns a mile off, and one could see miles of cabbage palms below like gigantic Turk's-head brooms, such as housemaids use to sweep away spiders with. The road along the coast to Kiama (pronounced *Kye-aye-mar*) was dreary enough, through miles of tall dead trees all ringed or burnt to death purposely by civilised man, who will repent some day when the country is all dried up, and grass refuses to grow any more.

At the lake of Illawarra we again found ourselves in the tropics, all tangled with unknown plants and greenery, abundant staghorns (*Platycerium* sp.), banksias, hakea, and odd things. I put up at the house of a pretty little widow, who apologised for having a party to say good-bye to some friend. They danced till morning, soon after which she was up to see me off. Before this I had wandered on the lovely sea sands, seeing and hearing the great waves as they dashed in and out of the blowholes. Rocks and giant fig trees grew close to its edge, and I found basalt pillars as sharply cut as any on the Giant's Causeway itself.

The road up the Kangaroo River and over the Sassafras Mountain is pretty. I tried to make out the sassafras leaves by their cinnamon scent, but nearly all the leaves were much scented on that road, and it was not till some time afterwards that I made out the tree. After turning the top of the hill we came suddenly on the zamia, or cycad – a most striking plant, with great cones standing straight up from the stem. When ripe, the segments turn bright scarlet, and the whole cone falls to pieces, then they split open and show seeds as large as acorns, from which a kind of arrowroot can be extracted, after washing out all the poison from it. The natives roast and eat the nut in the centre of the scarlet segments. There were no zamias outside that valley, which seemed to have no outlet. Like that of the Yosemite, it was discovered by a mere accident. It belonged, like the greater part of Illawarra, to the family of Osborne, who were building a large house there. It was certainly the most enticing part of Australia, and I wished I were an Osborne.

Charles Darwin, *The Voyage of the Beagle*, 1839

The climate here is damper than in New South Wales, and hence the land is more fertile. Agriculture flourishes; the cultivated fields look well, and the gardens abound with thriving vegetables and fruit-trees. Some of the farmhouses, situated in retired spots, had a very attractive appearance. The general aspect of the vegetation is similar to that of Australia; perhaps it is a little more green and cheerful; and the pasture between the trees rather more abundant. One day I took a long walk on the side of the bay opposite to the town: I crossed in a steamboat, two of which are constantly plying backwards and forwards. The machinery of one of these vessels was entirely manufactured in this colony, which, from its very foundation, then numbered only three and thirty years! Another day I ascended Mount Wellington; I took with me a guide, for I failed in a first attempt, from the thickness of the wood. Our guide, however, was a stupid fellow, and conducted us to the southern and damp side of the mountain, where the vegetation was very luxuriant; and where the labour of the ascent, from the number of rotten trunks, was almost as great as on a mountain in Tierra del Fuego or in Chiloe. It cost us five and a half hours of hard climbing before we reached the summit. In many parts the Eucalypti grew to a great size, and composed a noble forest. In some of the dampest ravines, tree-ferns flourished in an extraordinary manner; I saw one which must have been at least twenty feet high to the base of the fronds, and was in girth exactly six feet. The fronds forming the most elegant parasols, produced a gloomy shade, like that of the first hour of the night. The summit of the mountain is broad and flat, and is composed of huge angular masses of naked greenstone. Its elevation is 3100 feet above the level of the sea. The day was splendidly clear, and we enjoyed a most extensive view; to the north, the country appeared a mass of wooded mountains, of about the same height with that on which we were standing, and with an equally tame outline: to the south the broken land and water, forming many intricate bays, was mapped with clearness before us. After staying some hours on the summit, we found a better way to descend, but did not reach the Beagle till eight o'clock, after a severe day's work.

Mary Ann Parker, *A Voyage Round the World, in the Gorgon Man of War*, 1795

Upon our first arrival at *Paramatta*, I was surprised to find that so great a progress had been made in this new settlement, which contains above one thousand convicts, besides the military. There is a very good level road, of great breadth, that runs nearly a mile in a straight direction from the landing place to the Governor's house, which is a small convenient building, placed upon a gentle ascent, and surrounded by about a couple of acres of garden ground: this spot is called Rose-Hill. On both sides of the road are small thatched huts, at an equal distance from each other. After spending the day very agreeably at the Governor's, we repaired to the lodging which had been provided for us, where we had the comfort of a large wood fire, and found everything perfectly quiet, although surrounded by more than one thousand convicts. We enjoyed our night's repose; and in the morning without the previous aid of toilet or mirror, we set out for the Governor's to breakfast, and returned with the same party on the ensuing day.

This little excursion afforded us an opportunity of noticing the beautiful plumage of the birds in general, and of the *Emu* in particular, two of which we discovered in the woods: their plumage is remarkably fine, and rendered particularly curious, as each hen has two feathers generally of a light brown; the wings are so small as hardly to deserve the name; and, though incapable of flying, they can run with such swiftness that a greyhound can with difficulty keep pace with them. The flesh tastes some-what like beef.

In this cove there are some cool recesses, where with Captain Parker and the officers I have been many times revived after the intense heat of the day, taking with us what was necessary to quench our thirst. Here we have feasted upon Oysters just taken out of the sea;– the attention of our sailors, and their care in opening and placing them round their hats, in lieu of plates, by no means diminishing the satisfaction we had in eating them. Indeed, the Oysters here are both good and plentiful: I have purchased a large *three-quart* bowl of them, for a pound and a half of tobacco, besides having them opened for me into the bargain.

George Augustus Sala, *The Life and Adventures of George Augustus Sala*, 1895

I found Melbourne a really astonishing city, with broad streets full of handsome shops, and crowded with bustling, well-dressed people. For two days we held almost continuous receptions at the hotel; and I wish that I had preserved the hundreds of cards of the ladies and gentlemen who were so kind as to visit us. The next evening I lectured for two hours at the Town Hall, which was crowded, and the receipts amounted to more than £300. At the second lecture the aggregate takings were only £80. I am afraid, to begin with, that the hall was much too large for my purpose, and that my voice was scarcely audible to the occupants of the back seats. I remember at my first lecture being struck by two very curious circumstances. First, that what I intended to be a glowing eulogium on Mr. Gladstone was received in dead silence; and that every allusion I made to Lord Beaconsfield was responded to by a thunderous storm of hand-clapping and cheering.

Anthony Trollope, *Australia and New Zealand*, 1873

I visited Port Arthur, and was troubled by many reflections as to the future destiny of so remarkable a place. It is in a direct line not, I believe, above sixty miles from Hobart Town, but it can hardly be reached directly. The way to it is generally by water, and as there is no traffic to or from the place other than what is carried on by the government for the supply of the establishment, a sailing schooner is sufficient, – and indeed more than sufficiently expensive. In this schooner I was taken under the kind guidance of the premier and attorney-general of the island, who were called upon in the Performance of their duties to inspect the place

and hear complaints, – if complaints there were. We started at midnight, and as we were told at break of day that we had made only four miles down the bay, I began to fear that the expedition would be long. But the wind at last favoured us, and at about noon we were landed at Tasman peninsula in Norfolk Bay, and there we found the commandant of the establishment and horses to carry us whither we would. We found also a breakfast at the policeman's house, of which we were very much in want.

* * *

The scenery at this spot is very lovely, as the bright narrow sea runs up between two banks which are wooded down to the water. Then we went farther on, riding our horses where it was practicable to ride, and visited two wonders of the place, – the Blow-Hole, and Tasman's Aieh. The Blow-Hole is such a passage cut out by the sea through the rocks as I have known more than one on the west coast of Ireland under the name of puffing holes. This hole did not puff nor blow when I was there; but we were enabled by the quiescence of the sea to crawl about among the rocks, and enjoyed ourselves more than we should have done had the monster been in fall play. Tasman's Arch, a mile farther on, is certainly the grandest piece of rock construction I ever saw. The sea has made its way in through the rocks, forming a large pool or hole, some fifty yards from the outer cliffs, the descent into which is perpendicular all round; and over the aperture Stretches an immense natural arch, the Supports or side pillars of which are perpendicular. Very few even now visit Tasman's Arch; but when the convict establishment at Port Arthur comes to an end, as come to an end I think it must, no one will ever see the place. Nevertheless it is well worth seeing, as may probably be said of many glories of the earth which are altogether hidden from human eyes.

Arthur Conan Doyle, *The Wanderings of a Spiritualist*, 1921

On reaching Melbourne we were greeted at the station by a few devoted souls who had waited for two trains before they found us. Covered with the flowers which they had brought we drove to Menzies Hotel, whence we moved a few days later to a flat in the Grand, where we were destined to spend five eventful weeks. We found the atmosphere and general psychic conditions of Melbourne by no means as pleasant or receptive as those of Adelaide, but this of course was very welcome as the greater the darkness the more need of the light. If Spiritualism had been a popular cult in Australia there would have been no object in my visit. I was welcome enough as an individual, but by no means so as an emissary, and both the Churches and the Materialists, in most unnatural combination, had done their best to make the soil stony for me.

W.G. Grace, 'W.G.', *Cricketing Reminiscences and Personal Recollections*, 1899

Our match against twenty-two of Stawell began next morning, under conditions by no means inspiring. The ground was in a deplorable condition. Here and there were small patches of grass, but the greater part was utterly devoid of any herbage. We were not surprised to hear that the field had only been ploughed up three months before, and that the grass had been sown in view of our visit. The wicket was execrable, but there was no help for it – we had travelled seventy miles through bush and dust to play the match, and there was no option but to play.

Of course the cricket was shockingly poor, and the match a ludicrous farce. How bad the ground really was may be judged from the fact that one slow ball actually stuck in the dust, and never reached the batsman. It was ridiculous to play on such a wicket, but we were in for it and went through with it. Jupp and I batted first, and adopted slogging tactics. There was really nothing else to do, but the result was that in seventy minutes we were all out for 43 runs. If all the catches we gave had been held our total would have been still smaller. We were not sorry when our innings ended, as the wicket was one of the class which I have described, as bringing all players, good and bad, down to one level. Our opponents, who were more accustomed to such wickets, kept us in the field for a couple of hours, and made 71. McIntyre did the bowling for us, taking nine wickets for 10 runs. It is scarcely worth while recording the progress of the play, though it should be stated that we were beaten by ten wickets. A plague of flies, which swept over the field while play was in progress, added to our discomforts in this remarkable match.

Laurence Olivier, *Australian Journal*, 1946

April 14th.

Rude letters about 'Skin' in the press. After lunch to our great joy we were taken to a private collection of white kangaroos. They are Albinos. Vivien had seen kangaroos in Perth, but these were my first and I was ravished. People pointed out joeys that had just at that moment if only we hadn't missed jumped from the does' pouches. Just like Ruth Draper's garden. I took photos desperately but I know the light too bad for my sort of photography.

NEW ZEALAND

Mark Twain, *Following the Equator*, 1897

It was Junior England all the way to Christchurch – in fact, just a garden. And Christchurch is an English town, with an English-park annex, and a winding English brook just like the Avon – and named the Avon; but from a man, not from Shakespeare's river. Its grassy banks are bordered by the stateliest and most impressive weeping willows to be found in the world, I suppose. They continue the line of a great ancestor; they were grown from sprouts of the willow that sheltered Napoleon's grave in St. Helena. It is a settled old community, with all the serenities, the graces, the conveniences, and the comforts of the ideal home-life. If it had an established Church and social inequality it would be England over again with hardly a lack.

Lady Anne Barker, *Station Life in New Zealand*, 1870

You know we brought all our furniture out with us, and even papers for the rooms, just because we happened to have everything; but I should not recommend anyone to do so, for the expense of carriage, though moderate enough by sea (in a wool ship), is enormous as soon as it reaches Lyttleton, and goods have to be dragged up country by horses or bullocks. There are very good shops where you can buy everything, and besides these there are constant sales by auction where, I am told, furniture fetches a price sometimes under its English value. House rent about Christchurch is very high. We looked at some small houses in and about the suburbs of the town, when we were undecided about our plans, and were offered the most inconvenient little dwellings, with rooms which were scarcely bigger than cupboards, for 200 pounds a year; we saw nothing at a lower price than this, and any house of a better class, standing in a nicely arranged shrubbery, is at least 300 pounds per annum. Cab-hire is another thing which seems to me disproportionately dear, as horses are very cheap; there are no small fares, half-a-crown being the lowest 'legal tender' to a cabman; and I soon gave up returning visits when I found that to make a call in a Hansom three or four miles out of the little town cost one pound or one pound ten shillings, even remaining only a few minutes at the house.

All food (except mutton) appears to be as nearly as possible at London prices; but yet every one looks perfectly well-fed, and actual want is unknown. Wages of all sorts are high, and employment, a certainty.

ILLUSTRATIONS

All images © The British Library Board

p.2 Front Cover to *The Sphere* Orient Number, November 28, 1935. (HIU.LD48)

p.8 Detail from advertisement to 'Visit Egypt… 28 days of luxurious travel', *The Bystander*, September 25, 1929. (ZC.9.d.560)

p.11 Bedouin and Camels, from *The Travel Album of Count Ivan Forray*, 1857. (Tab.1237.a.)

p.13 The daughters of Suleyman Pasha in Cairo, from *The Travel Album of Count Ivan Forray*, 1857. (Tab.1237.a.)

p.14-15 Map of Africa, *from Le Grand Atlas, ou Cosmographie Blaviane* by Joan Blaeu, 1663. Maps C.5.b.1, Vol.10, pp.1-2

p.18 View on the Nile, Ferry to Gizeh', from *The Holy Land, Syria, Idumea, Arabia Egypt & Nubia* by David Roberts,1842-49. (746.e.7)

p.19 The Mountains of Samayut' drawn by Henry Salt, from *Twenty-four Views taken in St. Helena, the Cape, India, Ceylon, Abyssinia and Egypt*, 1809. (Maps 6.Tab.74)

p.20 A Street in Tangier', illustration by A.S. Forrest from *Peeps at Many Lands:Morocco* by John Finnemore, 1907. (010026.g.1/22)

p.25 A Bazaar, Marrakesh', illustration by A.S. Forrest from *Peeps at Many Lands:Morocco* by John Finnemore, 1907. (010026.g.1/22)

p.28 A Snake Charmer', illustration by A.S. Forrest from *Peeps at Many Lands:Morocco* by John Finnemore, 1908. (010026.g.1/22)

p.32 *Africa Tabula Geographica* by A.F. Zürner, c.1709. (Maps.K.Top.117.9)

p.38 Isfahan, from *Reise der K. Pruessischen Gesandtschaft nach Persien 1860 und 1861* by Heinrich Brugsch, 1862-63. (ORW.1986.a.1655)

p.40 Persepolis, from *Reizen over Moskovie, door Persie en Indie* by Cornelis de Bruyn, 1714. (10028.i.2)

p.42-43 *Tabula Nova Imperii Turcarum Arabum et Persarum* by Guillaume de L'Isle, c.1720. (Maps K.Top.113.5.1)

p.44 Damascus, from *Cairo, Jerusalem & Damascus: three chief cities of the Egyptian Sultans* by David Margoliouth, 1907. (K.T.C.107.a.10)

p.47 Pilgirms worshipping at the Ka'aba Mecca, miniature from a treatise on the law of religious observances by Abu Hanifah, produced in Southern Iran 1410-11. (Add. 27761, f.363)

p.48 The Ka'aba at Mecca, c.1880s, from *Bilder au Mekka* by C. Snouck Hurgronje, 1889. (X.463)

p.51 Photograph of T. E. Lawrence (Lawrence of Arabia), part of George Bernard Shaw's papers. (Add. 50584 A, photo 116)

p.52 Constantinople, from *Lewis's Illustrations of Constantinople* by John Frederick Lewis, 1838. (747.e.18)

p.54 Women taking recreation in a park, Turkish miniature, late 18th century. (Or. 7094, f.7)

p.56 Scutari, from *Lewis's Illustrations of Constantinople* by John Frederick Lewis, 1838. 747.e.18

p.58 The Gold Temple of the principal idol Guadma, taken from its front being the Eastern face of the Great Dagon Pagoda at Rangoon', from *Eighteen Views taken at or near Rangoon* by Joseph Moore, 1825. (Maps 15.e.26, plate 7)

p.60 The seven-headed snake of Nakhon wat [Angkor Wat], from *The Antiquities of Cambodia* by John Thomson, 1867. (Photo 983.(32.))

p.62-63 *A Map of the East Indies and the adjacent Countries: with the Settlements, Factoriers and Territories, explaining what belongs of England, Spain, France, Holland, Denmark, Portugal &c.* by Herman Moll, c.1710. (Maps.K.Top.115.6)

p.65 Miniature of the Polo brothers kneeling before the Great Khan, from the 'Voyages of Marco Polo' in a revised version attributed to Thibault de Cépoy, c.1340. (Royal 19 D.i, f.64r)

p.66 Playing Mah-jong, from *Nederlandsch Oost-Indischen Typen* by Auguste van Pers, 1854-56. (1781.c.23)

p.69 Map from *Peeps at Many Lands: The Gorgeous East. India, Burma, Ceylon and Siam* by Frank Elias, 1913. (010026.g.1/57)

p.70 'Cinghalese Sailing Canoe', from *Peeps at Many Lands: The Gorgeous East. India, Burma, Ceylon and Siam* by Frank Elias, 1913. (010026.g.1/57)

p.72 'A Hindu Maid', from *Peeps at Many Lands: The Gorgeous East. India, Burma, Ceylon and Siam* by Frank Elias, 1913. (010026.g.1/57)

p.76 View from Yokohama, from *A Series of 56 Views of Towns, Villages… in Japan* by W. Burger, 1871. (Maps 8.d.24.(45.))

p.78 The arrival of the Castilian envoy led by Don Clavijo before Timur at Samarkand. Mughal miniature fom *Malfuzat-i Timuri* [A History of Timur], 1800-1830. (Or. 158, f.322v)

p.80 View of the Graben in Vienna, etching and engraving by Johann Adam Delsenbach, 1719. (Maps K.Top.90.41-f)

p.82 Brussels, from *An Historical Account of the Campaign in the Netherlands, in 1815, under his Grace the Duke of Wellington, and Marshal Prince Blucher...* by William Mudford, 1817. (193.e.9)

p.84-85 *Cruchley's Enlarged Map of Europe*, 1851. (Maps Roll 167)

p.89 Illustration from *Homes of the Passing Show*, Savoy Press, 1900. (10350.dd.7)

p.91 Clovelly on the Coast of North Devon', engraving by William Daniell from *A Voyage round Great Britain undertaken in the summer of the year 1813* by Richard Ayton, 1814-25. (G.7043-6)

p.96 Lough Long, Western Highlands, Scotland', printed by F.J. Sarjent, 1811. (Maps K.top.49.36)

p.99 'Fine Weather', illustration from *The Illustrated London News*, March, 1887. (P.P.7611)

p.103 Zagreb, illustration from *Peeps at Many Lands: Yugoslavia* by Lena A Jovičič, 1928. (010026.h.1/11)

p.106 The Paris and London Steamer, illustration from *The Illustrated London News*, 1854. (P.P.7611)

p.108 Detail from *Plan de Paris. Commencé l'année 1734.* (Maps C.11.d.10)

p.110 Curious Menhir on the plain of Menec, bear Carnac', stereograph from *Narrative of a walking tour in Brittany* by John Mountenay Jephson, 1859. (10172.d.13)

p.113 A view of Notre Dame, *from Picturesque Architecture in Paris, Ghent, Antwerp, Rouen etc.* by Thomas Shotter Boys, 1839. (650.b.6)

p.117 View of the Cathedral Square in Cologne, engraving by Johann Ziegler, 1798. (Maps 6.Tab.12)

p.121 Budrum Castle, watercolour by R.P. Pullan, 1857, from a collection of drawings, plans and photographs of excavations at three sites in Greece. (Add. 31980 f.74)

p.125 View of the village of Glennan in the County of Ulster, 1771. (Maps K.Top.55.3)

p.126 Illustration from *Simplicissimus* 5th December, 1896. (LOU.F459) p.131 'Medieval Shop in Via Mattonata, Terracina', from *The Stones of Italy* by C. T. G. Formilli, 1927. (07816.c.51)

p.134 'Antiquarian Shop on the Ponte dei Dadi, Venice', from *The Stones of Italy* by C. T .G. Formilli, 1927. (07816.c.51)

p.136 Piazza and Church of Santa Maria Forisportam, Lucca, drawing by Bernardo Bellotto, 1742-1745. (Maps K Top 80.21-e)

p.140 St. Peter's Basilica, Vatican, Rome, from *Veduti di Roma* by Giovanni Battista Piranesi, 1762. (1899.h.12.(1.))

p.143 'Medieval House, Alatri', from *The Stones of Italy* by C. T .G. Formilli, 1927. (07816.c.51)

p.147 Lisbon, seen from the Quinta da Torrinha Val de Pereriro, drawn by L.B. Parkyns, engraved by W.J. Bennett, 1808-1817. (Maps K Top 74.66.c.3)

p.148 View of the Convent of St. Jerome of Belem and the entry into the Harbour at Lisbon, printed by Henri L'Evêque, 1816. (Maps K.Top.74.67.g)

p.150 The Plaza of Seville, from *Tauromachia; or the bull-fights of Spain* by Richard Ford, 1852. (C.52.I.2)

p.154-155 Glacier of the Rhône, from *Matériaux pour servir à létude des Glaciers* by Henri Hogard and Dollfus-Ausset, 1854. (Tab.583.b)

p.158 View of Stockholm taken from the Island of Langholm, printed by J. Mérigot, 1802. (Maps K.Top.111.107.b)

p.160-161 Map of Stockholm by J. B. Homann, 1720. (Maps K.Top.111.105)

p.164 The Niagara Falls, from *Treasure Spots of the World. A selection of the chief beauties and wonders of nature and art* by Walter B. Woodbury, 1875. (10028.g.5)

p.167 Columbus landing in America, from *America* by Theodor de Bry, 1634. (215.c.14.(1.))

p.178 'The Mountain Cabbage Palm on Palmeto', from *Drawings and sketches illustrating the scenery of the interior of British Guiana* by Edward A. Goodall, 1842-43. (Add. 16939, f.53)

p.182-183 *Totius Americae descriptio* by Nicolaes Visscher, c.1658. (Maps.K.Top.118.9)

p.186 Termite mounds, Sierra da Mantiquerra, Brazil, from *Expédition dans les parties centrales de l'Amérique du Sud, de Rio de Janeiro a Lima, et de Lima au Para* by F. L de Laporte, Count de Castelnau, 1843. (12915.i.1)

p.188 Ingenio Buena Vista, lithograph by Eduardo Laplante from *Los Ingenios. Coleccion de vistas de los principales ingenios de azucar de la Isla de Cuba* by Justo Cantero, 1857. (1780.c.14)

p.191 View of Port Antonio in the Parish of Portland, Jamaica, aquatint by J. Mérigot, 1800. (Maps.K.Top.123.55.f)

p.193 Rancheros, from *Voyage pittoresque et archéologique dans la partie la plus intéressante du Mexique* by Carl Nebel, 1836. (648.c.1)

p.194 The Ramparts of Mount Erebus, from *Scott's Last Expedition* by Leonard Huxley, 1913. (W3/2295)

p.196 The aurora australis or southern lights, from *The Heart of the Antarctic: being the story of the British Antarctic Expedition 1907-1909* by Ernest Shackleton, 1909. (2370.g.10)

p.197 Emperor Penguins, from *Scott's Last Expedition* by Leonard Huxley, 1913. (W3/2295)

p.198 Two Maoris, from *Sketches of scenery, portraits of natives, with representations of ceremonies, costume etc. in New Zealand* by Alexander Sinclair, Cuthbert Clarke & J. Merrett, 1842-1853. (Add. 19953, f. 60)

p.201 Map of Botany Bay in New South Wales made during Captain Cook's First Voyage, 1770. (Add. 31360, f.32)

p.202-203 Map of East India Isles and Australia, from *A General Atlas* by J. Wyld, c.1830. (Maps 44.e.4)

p.205 Rotomahana Lake New Zealand, drawn by Cuthbert Clarke, August 1850. (Add. 19954, f.30)

p.209 A fern tree, from *Sketches of scenery, portraits of natives, with representations of ceremonies, costume etc. in New Zealand* by Alexander Sinclair, Cuthbert Clarke & J. Merrett, 1842-1853. (Add. 19953, f. 101)

p.212 Sidney Cove, drawing made on 14th February 1800 from *Journal kept on board the Minerva Transport from Ireland to New-South Wales* by John Washington-Price, 1798-1800. (Add. 13880, f.79)

CREDITS

....

Every effort has been made to trace copyright holders and to obtain their permission for the use of copyright material. The publisher apologizes for any errors or omissions in the below list and would be grateful if notified of any corrections that should be incorporated in future reprints or editions of this book.